D0554858

Collector's Edition

THE
FOUR
DIMENSIONS
OF
PARADISE

FOR THE LIBRARY OF

January 1993

THE
FOUR DIMENSIONS OF
PARADISE

LITTERA SCRIPTA MANET

The Four Dimensions of PARADISE

BY

RABBI SAMUEL PENNER

In collaboration with and edited by
SHEBA PENNER

CYRUS PRESS

Acknowledgements

This book has been a labor of love and I wish to acknowledge all who have contributed from my wonderful daughter Eve and Rabbi Zalman Schachter Shalomi to my good friend Nancy Ann Tappe. Their direct contributions to the text as well as their emotional support throughout have been major. My special thanks to Kris Jeter and Alicia Magal for finding the jacket photographs, to Shendl Diamond for her calligraphy and to George Djordjevic for his exceptional design of the book. I would like to thank my publisher, Bill Gladstone of Cyrus Press, whose interest and commitment to this project has been steadfast and to his caring and efficient staff including Chris Johnson, Amy Davis, Dawn Carlin, Margot Maley, Lavender Ginsberg, Julie Castiglia and Carol Underwood.

Because this book has been so integral a part of my life I want to acknowledge all those friends who supported my husband's work while he was alive as well as those who have continued to support his life work since. Samuel's love of humanity motivated his scholarship and his writing and all who participate in its reading deserve acknowledgement as co-creators of this work. Thank you.

Book production and typography, book jacket, cover, interior of the book and all simulated woodcut decorations are designed and produced by George Djordjevic, of Djordjevic, Miller, Inc., Los Angeles.

ISBN 0-9627145-0-X

Library of Congress Catalog Card No. 92-074667

Printed in the United States of America

Publisher's Note

 t is with great pleasure that Cyrus Press inaugurates its publishing program with Rabbi Samuel Penner's THE FOUR DIMENSIONS OF PARADISE.

I first became aware of Rabbi Penner through his association with Jonas Salk on a project entitled THE EVOLUTION OF WISDOM. Samuel's untimely death prevented the completion of that book but fortunately Samuel did live long enough to nearly complete THE FOUR DIMENSIONS OF PARADISE. Ironically, the one section of THE FOUR DIMENSIONS OF PARADISE that Samuel did not complete was the section on mysticism. When Samuel's widow, Sheba brought the manuscript to me, I imagined that it would be necessary to find a scholar capable of writing the section on mysticism. To my surprise and delight, this was not necessary. Samuel had written the other sections in such a way that the reader's mystical relationship is illumined throughout providing a complete journey with Samuel's writing alone.

In discussing the manuscript and plans for publication with Sheba, we decided to add quotes from other thinkers, poets, writers and philosophers which would place Samuel's message in the broadest possible context. Samuel was a Rabbi but his teachings were universal. The truths revealed through a four dimensional understanding of biblical literature, in the Jewish

Kabbalah and in the practice of active participation in living in the FOUR DIMENSIONS OF PARADISE on a daily basis are reflected in the truths and ethical practices of all religions, sciences, arts and literatures. The selection of the quotes is Sheba's and she has done a remarkable job of not only selecting quotes but of placing them appropriately throughout Samuel's text to stimulate each reader's journey through the four dimensions. Given the similarities of Samuel's and Sheba's intellectual and artistic sensibilities as well as their spiritual and emotional union, I am quite certain that Samuel would have approved of Sheba's selections.

It is my fondest hope that all readers of THE FOUR DIMENSIONS OF PARADISE will enjoy Samuel's wit, wisdom and warmth as much as his friends did while he was alive. Samuel was a remarkable man and THE FOUR DIMENSIONS OF PARADISE is a fitting tribute to his life. Samuel's goal was to write an accessible yet enduring practical guide to living a spiritually balanced life in harmony with men and women of good will and the forces that shape our collective destiny and that of our planet. Samuel was a man of peace and love and it is the publisher's hope that you will join his ongoing journey through your reading of THE FOUR DIMENSIONS OF PARADISE and share the joy that continues to reverberate from his soul.

William Gladstone, Publisher

Preface

To fully appreciate universal mythologies, one must seek their deeper meaning on many levels. The Four Dimensions of Paradise seeks to make the multidimensional Bible literature available to all. By mapping for the reader, four specific dimensions to touch the mind, aesthetic and moral sense, heart, and the deeper soul, the reader is drawn in and engaged in an intimate interaction with this timeless ancient literature.

Further, it opens the possibility of seeing many aspects of one's own life in subtle multidimensions. One can apply these concepts to nature, the universe and our God. Seeing beyond the surface to these deeper levels offers an opportunity to sharpen our awareness and to enrich our gift of life.

As you open your mind and your heart to the warmth, information and humor in these pages you are also sure to find a very personal dimension that it touches.

Some of the truisms it contains can be found echoed in other religions, philosophies, literature and poetry. Consequently, several quotes have been chosen from different sources as examples of their timeless quality. I am sure you will find many of your own that you may choose to add in the blank pages provided for you throughout the book. It will be these personal observations, thoughts and feelings that you record into the blank pages that will make this book uniquely yours. It will be unlike any other copy. Become immersed as you allow yourself to be captivated by and to participate in the journey of THE FOUR DIMENSIONS OF PARADISE. It has the potential to serve as a guide to enrich, ennoble and empower all who choose to use this book for the affirmation and enrichment of all life.

Sheba Penner

Foreword

This book welcomes you to a trip through some uncharted places but it's no fantasy voyage. A journey into the Four Dimensions of Paradise can transform your life or, at the very least, enrich it immensely. What, you have every reason to ask, makes this trip so special?

☙ 1. You will discover a profound vision developed by the mystics of Kabbalah and a way that prepares you and every human being to enter into direct communication with God. Most of us have grown up with the notion that God communicates His wisdom only to some chosen few. While such ideas of divine favoritism and spiritual elitism are recurrent themes in pagan mythology, the biblical talmudic kabbalistic tradition opened up divine inspiration democratically to everybody.

On this trip, you will explore beyond the constricted world most of us inhabit and extend your consciousness into higher levels of experience, where evolved souls and creative spirits have always found nourishment, wisdom and more: ecstatic joy in reciprocal communication with God.

Maybe you feel uncomfortable with that. What will I say to God? The story is told of a minister who prayed all his life to be worthy of God's presence. One night, in his study, he heard a rustling of the wind and suddenly the whole room was charged with powerful vibrations. In a cold sweat, he phoned his bishop and whispered:

I think God is here in my study. What should I do?
Calmly the bishop answered: *Look busy!*

But what if you're not into any God belief? Don't let

that deter you from this trip. I find that those labels we pin on ourselves --religious,sceptic, agnostic,atheist - tell us very little about true spirituality. In all the old Scripture from Genesis to Chronicles, there is not one commandment: thus shalt thou believe. Not your professed creed but your actual deeds, your real lifestyle is what counts.

In the semantics of the Four Dimensions, all of human growth and achievement is the fruit of an evolving inter communication between the Creator and His human creatures. The scientist, the artist, the philosopher, the mystic and the humblest worker, all of us draw our inspiration from the infinite source of all wisdom. We will probe deeply into the nature of that communications system during your journey. Its purpose is to expand the horizons of your life, enlarge the perception of your options and challenge you to confront them.

❧ 2. You will be introduced to the most comprehensive and meaningful technique ever developed for understanding the Bible. These Four Dimensions of Paradise make a signal contribution toward revitalizing the whole field of modern biblical study. Distorted on the one hand by a simplistic, stifling fundamentalism and emasculated, on the other, by the imbalance of an exclusively empirical scholarship, Scripture needs to be restored to its authentic role: to serve as a full, four dimensional channel for the unimpeded flow of divine wisdom to all.

With its broad theory of multi-dimensional interpretations that draws upon the genius of a hundred generations in scriptural traditions, the Four Dimensions of Paradise opens up the Bible to you and to everyone, as originally intended. No human life is excluded from its treasure or from its power to inspire growth and ennoblement.

Your voyage into these four dimensions of the biblical world takes on a significance beyond your own personal enrichment. It equips you to play a greater role in that sacred evolutionary process creating on earth a paradisian harmony that unites nature and society, humanity and God.

🕊 3. Most precious among your encounters on this journey will be a philosophy of life, noble in concept and application. The distilled wisdom of millennia is brought together here from many sources to engage all who search for meaning, who yearn for an end to despair.

You will confront not only a theoretical wisdom but also a practical gage for measuring your personal evolution as a human being. How far have you come in cultivating your humanity? What levels are still unrealized? I hadn't planned it that way, but this book may well turn out to be your ultimate self-help book!

Some two centuries ago in czarist Russia, a venerable sage and mystic was imprisoned unjustly. The warden, a man who prided himself on his knowledge of Bible, would often come to visit and discuss Scripture with his famous prisoner. One day he asked:

How is it, after Adam had eaten the forbidden fruit in the Garden of Eden and had gone into hiding, that God comes looking for him and says: "Where are you?"

Didn't the omniscient God already know where Adam was hiding? The old sage smiled and said:

Every biblical word speaks to all people and to every age. Adam is more than the name of an individual, the progenitor of the human race. Adam means humanity. Thus God's question to him is really being addressed to you, the warden of this prison, right here and now. Where are you in your life? How are you using the precious years I give you to grow and develop yourself?

x

The Four Dimensions of Paradise contain no doctrinaire theory of self-actualization. They offer at first a new vocabulary for our generation. . . a vocabulary that maps out four illimitable dimensions of personal growth and evokes from you a response to the supreme question of your life: where are you?

And where are you going? Maybe you've given up too soon on yourself. You keep looking back to your past and see your life as wasted and unworthy. The vision of Pardes can illumine your way out of bondage to past frustration. It can also help you refocus your awareness of all the future possibilities yet within your grasp - your many new options for growth and the real joy of self-renewal. Wherever you are, you have a long and beautiful journey ahead.

Of course, the Four Dimensions offer much more than a felicitous vocabulary. They have something vital and compelling to say to you and to everyone of us who live in the twilight (Gotterdammerung) of all the ideological gods that failed.

An exquisite parable about Elijah says it best. We find him alone in a cave at Mt. Sinai, burnt out after all his heroic efforts to save his people from the oblivion cults of false gods they were into 28 centuries ago. Looking out over an awesome desert from the cave's entrance, he sees a vicious tornado ripping through the hills uprooting rocks and smashing them. But God's presence was not there among the howling winds. Next a deafening thunder and again God was not in the noise. Lightning flashes followed but no trace of God was in the flame. Finally the prophet hears a serene sound of stillness and knows that the God of truth is near.

Ideological clashes and revolutionary fury have enflamed our century; they have left us burnt out, aimless and despairing of hope for any real solutions or any

xi

meaning at all to the whole human-cosmic enterprise. We need to turn off the noise and listen for the still small voice that starts our journey inward... to probe the many dimensions of our divine essence, our latencies, capacities, aptitudes, talents and potentialities, physical and spiritual, all the abundant gifts of a generous Creator, and to begin developing them.

The thrust of your voyage through the Four Dimensions of Paradise is a search for balance between the internal and external. . .to make sure that the cultivation of your divine gifts will not end up as an exercise in narcissism. Too many movements for self-realization have degenerated into self idolatry cults. You and I can measure how far we have come on our journey by our readiness to reach out to others, to encourage their growth and advance thereby the renewal of society.

Underlying this whole system of ideas is the conviction that we can aspire on earth to experience the sublime joys of paradise in all its four dimensions. And each of us can serve as an important catalyst for that sacred work. But you don't have to wait until the end of days. The bliss of a journey through the Four Dimensions of Paradise is available now. This book gets you started.

No more than these few lines of prologue are needed to mark off some salient points on your voyage. The full meaning and significance of the Four Dimensions will be detailed in the body of our book. In essence, this prologue is my personal invitation to you to embark upon the most enchanting, refreshing and challenging journey you may ever make.

A master teacher suggested nearly 2,000 years ago:

*"It is not for you to finish the work,
nor are you free to abandon it."*

Table Of Contents

xiii

Introduction

systematic presentation of the Four Dimensions of Paradise is published for the first time in this book. Emerging in stages out of the mainstream of classic Hebrew learning and widely embraced by medieval Christian exegesis, this ancient vision was promulgated in its present form by the mystics of Kabbalah. I offer it here as a valuable guide for each of us on our journey to personal and social fulfillment on earth.

Why resurrect it now, seven centuries after its Kabbalistic formalization? Because I am convinced that its fuller meaning and significance have eluded us to this day and that these Four Dimensions of Paradise can open our generation of narrowing despair to a new enlargement of spirit and hope.

In vintage style, Mark Twain made this classic comment upon a verse in Psalms: "And Thou, O Lord, hast made man but a little lower than the angels..." adding, "and he's been gittin' a little lower ever since!"

That observation touches a raw nerve of truth. Our century has experienced signal breakthroughs in science and technology. We reach for the stars but our own planet is still convulsed with atavistic violence and accelerating crime, racial and national xenophobia, ecological devastation, massive hunger, war and genocide.

1

As we move into the last two decades of the twentieth century, we confront a rising callousness to human life, dignity and freedom. We are becoming inured to the hopeless, deadend impoverishment of vast populations and to the repression and pitiless torture of human beings.

A generation ago, farsighted playwrights of the Theatre of the Absurd portrayed what they intuited to be the zeitgeist of tomorrow. That tomorrow has arrived too soon vindicating their perception of society as a planetary theatre of the absurd. How mindlessly we adjust to the insane expenditure of our resources all over the earth, our time, energy, capital and labor, for newer life annihilating weaponry in an age of thermonuclear overkill. And who can make sense out of today's suicidal war against all life supporting systems on earth?

Symptomatic of all this madness is the utterly obscene revival of human slavery in our generation. So quickly has this modern plague of totalitarian enslavement infested the earth that free societies now constitute a mere minority of the world's population. What an ironic and counterrevolutionary erosion of all the hopes that stirred the leaders of the American Revolution only two centuries ago.

They were confidant with Patrick Henry that America had "lighted the candle to all the world"; with John Adams that "the Revolution was fought for future millions and millions of millions" and that "it would spread Liberty and Enlightenment everywhere in the world"; with Tom Paine that "we Americans have it in our power to begin the world again. . . the birthday of a new world is at hand"; with Thomas Jefferson, that "it is impossible not to be sensible that we are acting for all mankind"; and with Benjamin Franklin, master propagandist of the revolutionary movement, who proclaimed: "God grant

2

that not only the love of liberty, but thorough knowledge of the rights of man may pervade all the nations of the earth, so that a philosopher may set his foot anywhere on its surface and say 'this is my country'."

More than 3,000 years ago, in an age of unrelieved, bitter enslavement, the Jewish people stepped out to the center of the stage in human history with a new message of hope. They had experienced a signal liberation out of cruel bondage in Egypt, the most technically advanced society, and also, one of the most oppressive and death-oriented cultures of antiquity.

Their response in the Hebrew Scripture was a refreshingly joyful affirmation of life on earth and a new vision of the human potential for evolving a personal and societal life style of justice and compassion, love and dignity, freedom and equality, learning and nobility, joy and creativity, sanctity and peace.

Sharing in that old mythical legacy of a Golden Age at the dawn of history, the Jews could not accept its fatalistic corollary: the inexorable fall and descent of man ("gettin' a little lower ever since"). Instead they developed one of the most life nourishing concepts in the history of ideas: the messianic hope for a future redemption of Israel and all society... not in some other worldly paradise but right here on earth! Indispensable to that hope was the confidence in our capacity to achieve it, to transform our lives personally and socially in physical, mental and spiritual fulfillment.

The Baal Shem Tov summed up a major motif of biblical prophecy when he taught that the authentic vocation of a human being is "to serve as a vital link on the chain between Adam and the Messiah..." that is to say, between the creation and redemption of the human family. In this view, the whole of history is perceived as a drama of evolution, a journey from Paradise Lost to an even more resplendent Paradise Regained. That journey is both individual and communal; in fact, each interacts with the other organically.

Every person has an active role to play in advancing those "messianic days" of human fulfillment. All are summoned to socio-ethical responsibility according to the mainstream of biblical tradition. That call over the centuries has brought dignity into human lives and moved people to strive for higher self-evolvement. It has also inspired renewed courage and hope in moments of agonizing despair.

Our journey into the Four Dimensions of Paradise is rooted in these early biblical ideas and messianic yearnings. From antiquity to this day, Hebrew scholars never saw the Bible as a closed work, a finite repository of divine inspiration congealed forever by one authoritative imprimatur of truth. Not at all! They regarded it as an infinite and ongoing source of divine illumination. The Eternal Creator never stopped communicating with His creatures. His inspiration continues to engage us in every generation through the words of the Torah (biblical teaching). "Even if one person studies Torah, the Shekhinah (presence) of God is there with him."

In the first section of this work, which I have entitled, "A Guide For Your Earth Trip", we examine some core values of the biblical lifestyle. Our discussion is enriched with new insight from the cognate disciplines of archeology, comparative religion, mythology, history, semantics and philosophy. The central question we ask is this: what, if anything of significance, do these scriptural concepts, that have exerted in the past so powerful an influence upon our civilization, have to say to us today? I have focused upon those core values that speak to the affirmation of life, sanctifying, enjoying, appreciating, celebrating and ennobling it with learning and democratic commitment.

For those whose encounter with Scripture has been limited to occasional sectarian propaganda or less, the first section of this book may turn out to be somewhat traumatic. Voltaire's suggestion, that the Bible is far more celebrated than read, would be hard to refute today. There's a wonderful story told about a bar mitzvah reception to which three rabbis were invited. The Reform rabbi presented his gift to the young celebrant, a copy of the Bible. The Conservative rabbi brought an edition of the Bible with commentaries and the Orthodox rabbi brought an umbrella. When he was asked: What kind of bar mitzvah present is an umbrella?

He answered:

At least this one he will surely open!

Having opened the Bible at last and acquired from it some basic guidance for our earth trip, we turn our attention in the second section of this book to the Four Dimensions of Paradise.

What are they? Let me explain at first that the Hebrew equivalent for the Greek word, PARADISE, is PARDES. Since only the consonants in Hebrew are intrinsic, the four consonants PRDS, according to a passage in the Zoharic literature of Kabbalah (Jewish mysticism), form an acronym containing the first letters of the names for each of the four dimensions:

פ **P** shat   is the dimension of literal and objective truth.

ר **R** emez   designates the dimension of allegory and poetic truth.

ד **D** erasha refers to the dimension of ethical and homiletic truth.

ס **S** od   constitutes the dimension of mystical and metaphysical truth.

5

INTRODUCTION

The core of this book is the claim that these Four Dimensions of Paradise provide us with greater personal enrichment through:

1. A more comprehensive approach to the understanding of scriptural wisdom.
2. A more authentic way to enter into the eternal dialogue between God and humankind.
3. A more balanced philosophy of life and harmonious vision of human fulfillment.
4. A more practical application of The Four Dimensions of Paradise to bring about a more harmonious integration of the physical, mental, emotional and spiritual aspects of life.

Quite a claim! But it is all implicit in the earliest Kabbalistic formulation of the Pardes, which held that those, who master the four dimensions of biblical communication, enter the eternal life of Paradise and enjoy direct communion with the Shekhinah, the immanent presence of God. We will examine the roots of this idea in pre-Kabbalistic thought and, transposing it into a modern key, assess its contemporary significance.

In what may turn out to be the most valued part of the book, we explore the unfamiliar Hibraic literary world of Midrash, Talmud and Kabbalah, under the subtitle "Creative Exploration in Four Dimensions". Selections from this massive post-biblical literature will demonstrate the techniques of exposition by which a single biblical word or phrase can be illumined with a wealth of new insights, meanings, suggestions, nuances and overtones in all four dimensions. We touch here what I perceive to be the authentic record of an extraordinary dialogue between a people and God over the millennia.

Of course, the use of allegorical and other modes of

interpretation was by no means exclusive to Hebrew culture. Greek philosophers allegorized the old Homeric epics and many other literary classics quite liberally in order to interpret their ideas in greater consonance with contemporary thought.

With the rise of Christianity, the early Church fathers and their medieval heirs made extensive use of allegory, homily and mysticism in their canonical and extra-canonical writings. The four dimensions were well known to medieval Christian scholars but they did not for the most part think highly of the first dimension of literal or objective meaning.

Several centuries later after the birth of Islam, the early expounders of Hadith, the Mohammedan oral tradition of interpreting the Koran (Kitab-Holy Writ) of the prophet's revelations, renewed the ancient exegetical methods of the Hebrew sages. Their interpretations developed Islamic law (Shari'a) and lore in modalities remarkably parallel to the classic evolution of Jewish hermeneutics.

Intriguing though it be, we cannot do justice within the scope of this one study to so extensive a subject as the way of the four dimensions in Christian and Islamic literature. That must await substantive treatment in the future. Here we can only call attention to the fact of significant cultural exchange across clearly demarcated religious lines in the classic medieval world, even to the extent of sharing methods as well as ideas.

Which brings me to an important idea about the approach of this book and the spirit that animates it. When the Nobel Prize for Literature was awarded to the American novelist, William Faulkner, he was told: "You created out of the State of Mississippi one of the landmarks of twentieth century world literature". Strange praise. In all his novels, Faulkner rarely

ventured beyond the borders of one county in Mississippi. Yet, so far from becoming a parochial writer, he
succeeded in making a rich contribution to world literature. How is that possible? Because by digging deeply
into his own roots, his native soil and authentic legacy,
he could discover the universal truths that enrich all
people.

The luminous vision of the Four Dimensions of Paradise reaches out to the whole human family. Yet its roots
take us deeply into the Kabbalah tradition of Jewish
mysticism that goes back to the earliest books of the
Hebrew Bible some 4,000 years ago. Nor is there anything anomalous about that. For the noblest contributions of biblical and postbiblical Hebrew literature were
never limited parochially to the Jewish people but were
extended to everyone. "All the teachings of Torah (the
collective Jewish legacy) were given to ennoble the human race."

The Four Dimensions of Pardes, crowning achievement of Kabbalah, is an authentic expression of Jewish
spirituality precisely because it has something vital to
say to each of us on earth. Individually and collectively
it supplies us with guidance and energy for a paradigmatic shift to more enriched living.

"Who is wise? Those who learn from everyone," said
an ancient sage, which I take to mean -- those who are
open to the wisdom of every tradition: cultural, spiritual and ethnic. Openness of mind, heart, soul and
spirit, that is the key to wisdom and to life itself. How
fascinating that the old perception is now confirmed
by our most advanced scientific thought, which understands life as an open system and death as a closed
system. But more of that later on.

Turning to the final section of this book, we will
discover, upon close examination of the Four Dimensions of Paradise, not only a remarkably fresh and open-

ended approach to scriptural understanding, but also an expanded awareness of the creative possibilities of human life. Ideas, like living seed, contain an unpredictable latency for growth and quite often flower in new times and circumstances with surprising vigor.

I want to share with you in the closing chapters of this book some nourishing ideas encountered along the four ways of Pardes. They run counter to the accelerating dehumanization of our time. And they suggest that Orwell's nightmare of robotized neo-slavery is not our inevitable fate; alternatives of wisdom, compassion, freedom, joy and dignity are still available.

This wisdom of the Four Dimensions of Paradise challenges you to understand yourself, get into your cells, discover who you are and what you are doing here on earth. It will also help you see some of the untapped potential within you. So many of us go through our few years on this planet mindless of our real gifts of mind and heart, imagination and spirit, character and personality, mindless and also joyless, for there is no joy without growth and self-realization.

Strangers to ourselves, how can we relate successfully to others? The accumulated wisdom of millennia is encapsulated in Pardes to offer guidelines on what it means to evolve as a human being (a mensch) in all our interrelationships - at home, at work and in the community.

And our possibilities for self-cultivation reach even higher. For we are all formed out of the same matter as the stars and the range of your vision sets the boundaries of your life. An old folk tale has it that "a worm creeps into the horseradish and eyes tearing and burning, thinks it's the whole universe." We tiny specks on an embarrassingly small planet revolving around a tenth rate sun among trillions of other sun stars in our galaxy, which is only one of some 10 billion more galaxies all moving with inconceivable speed in every direction – how many of us live out our lives like that worm?

The way of the four dimensions expands our awareness of the universe and its Creator. The scientifically known is no less wondrous than the unfathomed mystery and both are essential to the growth of an authentic human being.

If I were asked to sum up in one phrase the value of this journey through the Four Dimensions of Paradise, I would answer with Ezekiel's line:

"And I will give you a new heart and a new spirit will I put into you. I'll remove the heart of stone from your body and replace it with a heart of flesh."

The individual is capable both of enobling life and disfiguring it. Basic purpose and human destiny are not without but within. -- Norman Cousins

In what area has your heart or spirit become hardened?
How can you begin to change this?

BOOK ONE

A Guide For Your Earth Trip

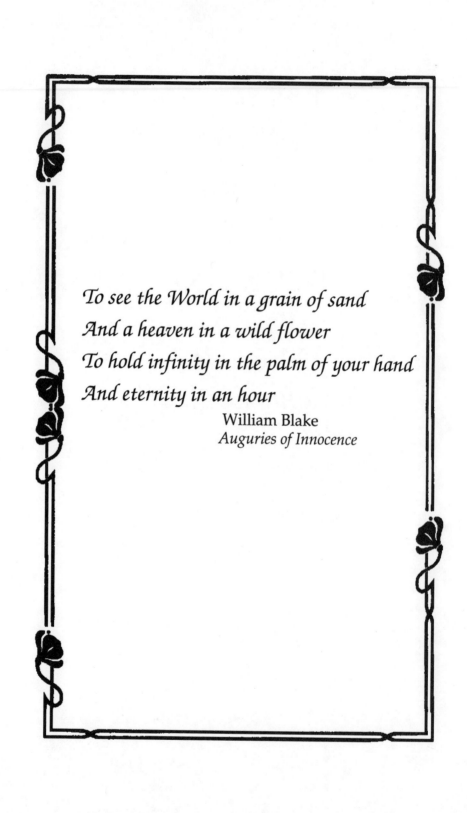

To see the World in a grain of sand
And a heaven in a wild flower
To hold infinity in the palm of your hand
And eternity in an hour

William Blake
Auguries of Innocence

1. Affirming Life

delightful story was told by the talmudic sage, Rabbi Joshua ben Levi. "When Moses went on high, the angels said to the Holy One Blessed Be He:

~Lord of the universe, what is a mortal doing in our midst?

~He's come to receive the Torah, answered the Eternal.

~What, they argued? Your most precious treasure, concealed for a thousand generations, you give to a creature of flesh and blood? Is it not written: 'Lord, our God, how great is Your name in all the earth and Your glory spread over the heavens...what is man that You remember him or the son of man that You take account of him'?

Then the Holy One Blessed Be He turned to Moses and said:

~Answer them.

~I'm worried, said Moses, that they may wipe me out with the flame of their breath.

~Hold on to my Throne of Glory, said the Eternal, and answer them.

~Lord of the universe, Moses began, this Torah that You are giving me, what is written in it? I am the Lord Your God Who took you out of the land of

Egypt, the house of bondage.' Were these angels
in Pharaoh's Egypt? Did they suffer the bitterness of slavery? What need do they have for
Torah? And what else is written? 'Remember the
Sabbath to keep it holy.' When do these angels
work that they require Sabbath rest? What more
is written? "Honor your father and mother.' Do
they have parents who need their loving
concern? And what else is written? 'You shall
not murder. . .You shall not commit adultery...
You shall not steal.' Do these angels experience
jealousy or lust?"

Evidently the angels were convinced by his compelling arguments, according to the story, which ends by
describing how they praised God for His good judgment
and presented Moses with many gifts.

This legendary gem is a prototype of the literary
genre, agada, the interpretive story in post biblical
Jewish literature, which captures the heart with its
imaginative and disarmingly simple style but also
penetrates the mind with profound instruction.

It raises a very basic question: where can we humans
find guidance for self-growth? Unlike angels, we are
imperfect creatures, heirs to primal instincts of hunger,
lust, fear and envy. All of us stand in need of effective
enlightenment to help us rechannel our primitive,
destructive instincts into new modalities of life enhancement.

The inspired guide according to this agada is Torah,
the Teaching, "whose ways are beautiful and whose paths
all lead to peace." The Hebrew word for peace, shalom,
means much more than peace; it derives from a semantic
root connoting wholeness and fulfillment.

"More precious than the rarest of gold," rhapsodizes
the poet of Psalms, "the Torah of God is integrally pure,
refreshing the soul." Rashi, the Hebrew commentator

par excellence of Scripture, caught the double entendre of this participal clause, "meshivat nefesh," which also means "turning the soul." Choosing the latter meaning, he explains the verse to signify that Torah possesses full power to redirect the soul away from destruction to life.

He is right. The quintessence of Torah is the affirming of life on earth, consecrating, celebrating and renewing it; and that has remained a major motif of Jewish tradition to this day.

You may ask: is it really so extraordinary for a religious tradition to be life affirming? The answer is yes! A well known principle in the philosophy of logic suggests that to understand in depth what an idea affirms you must explore what it negates. What makes the Hebrew affirmation of life on earth so revolutionary can best be grasped by examining alternative religious views and lifestyles.

The essential misery of earthly existence is the cornerstone of ancient Indian religion and philosophy. Its highest sancta were expressed in renouncing life. India became the great teacher of asceticism to the world.

The classic Hindu Brahman ideal became schematized in four stages of life. The first is the life of the student attached to his teacher and learning the Vedas. The second is the life of the householder, who marries, starts a family and honors his obligation to the gods. The third is the life of the hermit, who abandons home and family for the forest, where he practices ascetic austerities vigorously; he no longer performs most of the sacrifices to the gods but reflects on their mystical meaning. The fourth and highest stage is the life of the ascetic, who goes alone, without companions, without fire, without a home. He will live among the roots of trees, possessing only a bowl, a stick, a water jug and begging for food. He will be utterly detached and indifferent, desiring neither life nor death, a sannyasi,

15

one who has given up everything and devotes himself to spiritual meditation. That is the supreme achievement of sanctity in the Hindu tradition.

The reform movement of Buddhism sought a middle way between the extremes of self mortification and self indulgence. In Buddha's discourse with the five ascetics, known as the Sermon at Benares, the enlightened master offers his famous remedy for the misery of existence. Even as the physician proceeds medically in four steps: to diagnose the nature of the disease, trace its etiology, remove the cause and present the cure, so Buddha offers therapy to the ailing soul of humankind with his Four Great Certainties and consequent Eightfold path.

The Four Great Certainties or Noble Truths are:

1. The universality of suffering. Birth is suffering, age is suffering, illness is suffering, death is suffering; contact with what we dislike is suffering, separation from what we like is suffering, failure to attain what we crave is suffering… in brief, all that makes bodily existence is suffering.

2. The etiological cause for all this suffering is desire, the lust for sensuous pleasures, the desire for life, the craving for health. This craving, which entraps us in the karmic cycle of birth, death, and rebirth is the universal cause of suffering.

3. The way to end suffering is to extricate its cause, tear all desire out by the roots, free oneself from the world of the senses, from the sense of self, from the wheel of life, i.e., to achieve nirvana, which literally means the blowing out, as of a candle, the extinction of physical existence.

4. The way to attain this blessed therapy of total release is through the Eightfold Path, which consists of right belief, right resolution, right

16

speech, right conduct, right means of subsistence, right effort, right meditation and right absorption.

The reader is cautioned against a simplistic reading of these basic doctrines of the Buddha. They are developed, explicated and applied with great subtlety and depth, requiring detailed study. Here they are merely listed to convey the mood of negating earthly existence that surrounds this system of thought. Although the Buddha held excessive fasting and self-mortification to be unprofitable, his ideology and the missionary movement of monastic asceticism he founded espoused a renunciation of physical life. The persuasive thrust of this asceticism reached out, not only to the Far East, but also to western religion and philosophy.

We are not accustomed to associate asceticism with Hellenistic civilization. Yet the mystery religions of Greece and Rome were saturated with a dualistic view of materiality as unclean vis-a-vis the purity of the spiritual; they were also filled with rituals of self-mortification to achieve eligibility in an undefiled, other-worldly salvation.

Greek Orphism typifies the glorification of the ascetic way of life. It held that "the source of evil lay in the body with its appetites and passions, which must therefore be subdued if we are to rise to the heights which is in us to attain... the belief behind it is that this present life is for the soul a punishment for previous sin, and the punishment consists precisely in this, that it is fettered to a body. This is its calamity and is compared sometimes to being shut up in a prison, more times to being buried in a tomb."

Platonic philosophy shows strong Orphic influences. It too is permeated with a sharp dualism. Matter is evil for it resists the Idea, the perfect form. The soul is entombed, encaged in the body; it desires always to

17

escape and return to its true home with God. Only death can give the soul a chance to discover pure knowledge and real happiness "For the body is the source of endless trouble to us by reason of the mere requirement of food; and is liable also to diseases which overtake and impede us in the search after true being. It fills us full of loves, and lusts, and fears, and fancies of all kinds, and endless foolery, and in fact, as men say, takes away from us the power of thinking at all...and, last and worst of all, even if we are at leisure and betake ourselves to some speculation, the body is always breaking in upon us, causing turmoil and confusion in our enquiries, and so amazing us that we are prevented from seeing the truth. It has been proved to us that, if we would have pure knowledge of anything, we must be quit of the body– the soul in herself must behold things in themselves; and then we shall attain the wisdom which we desire, and of which we say that we are lovers; not while we live but after death. In this present life, I reckon that we make the nearest approach to knowledge when we have the least possible intercourse or communion with the body, and we are not surfeited with bodily nature, but keep ourselves pure until the hour when God himself is pleased to release us. And thus having got rid of the foolishness of the body, we shall be pure and hold converse with the pure, and know of ourselves the clear light everywhere, which is no other than the light of truth."

The Eleusinian mysteries, Pythagoreanism, Cynicism, NeoPythagoreanism, Neoplatonism, Mithraism and the Gnostic mystical theosophies in the first centuries of the common era, all shared in that weltanschauung, the world outlook of asceticism, which Christianity inherited in its earliest development.

The New Testament abounds in condemnation of

the flesh, the material pleasures of physical life. "They that are of Christ have crucified the flesh with its affections and lusts...Walk in the Spirit and you shall not fulfill the lusts of the flesh. For the flesh lusts against the Spirit and the Spirit against the flesh."

The inexorable consequence of that crucifixion of the flesh was the idealization of celibacy. "The children of this world marry and are given in marriage. But they which shall be accounted worthy to obtain that world, and the resurrection of the dead, neither marry nor are given in marriage ."

Paul reinforces the ideal of celibacy. "I say therefore to the unmarried and widows, it is good for them to abide (celibate) even as I. But if they cannot contain, let them marry; for it is better to marry than to burn."

The life of poverty and suffering was extolled in early Christian doctrine. True believers in Christ, according to Paul, should "suffer with him, that we may be glorified together." The salvational style of ascetic mortification gave rise in medieval Christendom to hermitages, monasteries, nunneries, and to congeries of religious orders, itinerant beggars, saints living in caves and deserts; Stylites living on solitary mountain tops and pillars; Dendrites inhabiting trees; Catenati living in heavy chains; Hebdomadarii taking food only once a week (the ultimate diet) and Flagellants seeking penance by whiplash.

By no means was the penitential value of self-denial and suffering limited to the saints, but commended to all the faithful. "Blessed be you poor for yours is the kingdom of God, Blessed are you that hunger now for you shall be filled. Blessed are you that weep now for you shall laugh. . . for behold your reward is great in heaven. . . But woe unto you that are rich for you have received your consolation. Woe unto you that are full

19

for you shall hunger. Woe unto you that laugh now for you shall mourn and weep." Most crucial to the beginnings of Christianity is the focus placed, not on this world, but on the other wordly kingdom. "My kingdom is not of this world."

The mood of Christian thought and lifestyle retained its ascetic modalities of seclusion, retreat, penance, poverty, suffering and renunciation of earthly pleasures for the sake of other worldly redemption, even after the Constantinian integration of church and state. Its central drama featured the individual soul striving for a heavenly salvation unattainable on earth.

In all fairness, we should note that modern movements in Christianity, within the Roman Catholic Church and among many Protestant denominations, have transcended those old modalities of thought and lifestyle. So far from renunciation or rejection, they are confronting the issues and responding to the challenges of enriching life on earth. As Reinhold Niebuhr and other modern Christian theologians have pointed out, this social-moral activism, so rare in the great spiritual traditions of India, is an authentic part of the Christian legacy that goes back to Sinai and the messianic passion of biblical prophecy. Embedded in the earliest roots of Christianity is a sensitive concern, a pastoral caring for human needs in this world.

What strikes us as refreshing in the Hebraic biblical tradition is its intense and uncompromised affirmation of life on earth. The essential goodness of the physical world is asserted forcefully in the very first chapter of Genesis. A refrain complements God's creation of the material universe day by day assuring us, "And the Lord saw that it was good." As if to settle any lingering doubts on this matter, Scripture concludes the sixth day of creation, when man and the animals were called into being, with the verse: "And the Lord saw all that He had done and behold it was very good."

Everything created by the Eternal, physical and spiritual, is worthy of sanctification. From Genesis to Chronicles, Hebrew Scripture rejects all forms of dualism as inconsistent with the unity of God. A talmudic sage made the bold assertion that even the sexual drive is included in the divine judgment of creation as "very good." Why? Because without it, "no man would build a home, take a wife or beget children."

The body is not the enemy but the sanctuary of the soul. It reflects the marvelous handiwork of a loving Creator and deserves to be tendered with loving care. The story is told of the immortal Hillel who, upon taking leave of his students, was asked by them:

~Rabbi, where are you going?

~To perform a mitzvah.

~And what is this mitzvah?

~To wash my body in the bathhouse.

~Is this really a mitzvah (a commandment of the Torah, an essential practice of Judaism)?

~Most assuredly yes! the master replied. Regard the emperor's statues standing in Roman theatres and stadiums. An official is appointed to take care of them, to scour and rinse them, for which he is well compensated and honored. . . How much more should I, created in God's image, cleanse my body, His divine creation."

Hebrew scriptural teachings never viewed the human body as being sanctified by physical suffering, celibacy or renunciation. There is not a single commandment among all the 613 in the Torah, which requires the mortification of the flesh. One mitzvah does call for the public fast of the Day of Atonement, the Sabbath of

Sabbaths; its meaning was immortalized in Isaiah's cadences, read in all synagogues during that most sacred day:

> *"Is it to bow low like a bulrush*
> *And spread sackloth and ashes?*
> *Will you call this a fast day*
> *Acceptable to God?*
>
> *This is the fast I choose:*
> *To loose the bands of wickedness,*
> *To undo the thongs of the yoke,*
> *To liberate all the oppressed*
> *And break open every bond*
> *To share your bread with the hungry*
> *And welcome the homeless, the poor into your home*
> *When you encounter the naked to clothe them*
> *And never hide yourself from your own flesh."*

The value of occasional fasting was recognized but its excessive use, as a path to holiness, was condemned. "All who afflict themselves with incessant fasting are called sinners," claims an authoritative talmudic text; a cognate teaching explains that "the merit of observing a fast day lies in the charity we give to the poor."

Of course, Jews always had their ascetics. Nazirites are mentioned in Mosaic law. Samson was a Nazirite; his Biblical portraiture is a pathetic exposure of the antihero, who turns out to be nothing more than a muscle-bound schlemiel. Jeremiah dialogued with the Rehabites, a community of tent-dwellers, who sought refuge from decadent urban life some 2,500 years ago. During the latter days of the second Jewish state, the ascetic movements of the Therapeutae, Essenes, Qumran Dead Sea Commune, Damascus Sect, early Palestinian church and others were all part of a remarkable period of religious fermentation and experimentation.

22

We are astonished to discover in one of the Dead Sea Scrolls, the Manual of Discipline, the constitution of a Jewish monastic community 2,100 years ago in Israel, which is an early prototype of the medieval Christian monastery, even to the name of its leader: episcopos, the Greek term for bishop. Surely then, the pages of Jewish history down to modern times are not lacking in Jewish mystics, both individuals and groups, who were attracted to the ascetic life.

What stands out significantly is that these were all minority dissident movements unaccepted by the mainstream tradition! It could not be otherwise. Biblical and post-biblical Judaism had achieved *(ab initio)* a vigorous commitment to life. "I place before you this day the choice between life and death, the blessing or the curse; choose, therefore, life that you and your children may live."

That life affirmation extended beyond the parameters of faith. It involved one's daily lifestyle, the way we relate to ourselves, our family, friends, and community. The emphasis was never upon a mere confession of creed but always upon the active implementation of your love of God: "to walk in His ways and fulfill His teachings, laws and statutes." Faith, in classical Torah, cannot be confined to theological speculation and the articulation of faith offers no theological formula for instant salvation. We measure our faith by the deeds we perform every day. The ancient Hebrew prophet said it best: "A righteous man lives by his faith."

23

By having reverence for life, we enter into a spiritual relation with the world.

By practicing reverence for life we become good, deep and alive.

Albert Schweitzer

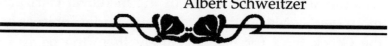

All of Schopenhauer's hate for Judaism and the Jews... arose largely from the fact that he could not forgive Judaism for it's affirmation of life. Klausher, from Jesus to Paul

2. Sanctifying Life

When the Infinite One planned to reveal Himself and give the Torah Tablets to Israel, He did not go to Israel at first but to all the other nations. He went to the children of Esau and said to them:

~Will you accept the Torah?

~What's written in it?, they asked.

~You shall not murder, He answered.

~Master of the Universe, they said, we have an ancestral tradition to live by the sword. Sorry, we cannot accept your Torah.

So He went to the Ammonites and the Moabites and asked them:

~Will you accept the Torah?

~What's in it?

~You shall not commit adultery.

~But that's our favorite national pastime. No, your Torah is not for us.

So He went to the Ishmaelites and said to them:

~Will you accept the Torah?

~What's in it?

~You shall not steal.

~Sovereign of the Universe, how will we make our living?

The Eternal approached every nation asking them if they wanted the Torah. Everyone refused. Finally He

25

came to the Israelites at Sinai and offered them the Torah. And they answered:

~Everything the Eternal has proclaimed we will perform."

Another ending to this classic midrashic story was suggested by a contemporary humorist to the effect that, when the Lord came to the Jews at Sinai and offered the Torah, they asked:

~What does it cost?

~The Tablets of the Torah are free, absolutely free, said the Eternal.

~O.K., so we'll take two tablets!

The Talmud, however, suggests a much more profound ending to this legend. In that version, the Jews didn't want the Torah any more than all the others. "So the Holy One Blessed Be He lifted up Mt. Sinai and suspended it over them, like a tank, and threatened them:

~Accept this Torah or this place will be your grave!"

At the core of that agadic masterpiece we find a perceptive commentary upon the nature and role of Torah. Once and for all, it lays to rest the gross distortion of the "chosen people" concept. Many centuries earlier the Hebrew prophet Amos had clarified the matter in immortal lines:

"To Me, you Israelites are no better than the Ethiopian blacks, saith the Lord. I brought Israel out of the land of Egypt but also the Philistines out of Capthor, and the Arameans out of Kir."

There are no favorites before God. The rabbinic legend above expanded that idea. Israel was not the first but the last to be offered the Torah. What counted supremely was not who were chosen, but who chose to commit themselves to the covenant of Torah.

What makes this Torah covenant so noteworthy? It started a revolutionary spiritual-ethical experiment so avant-garde that nobody was ready to accept it 3,500 years ago.

Not even the Jews! Forty days, after their Sinaitic commitment, they retrogress to the primitive worship of a golden calf so familiar to them in Egypt. Centuries of prophetic teachers excoriate them for violating the Torah covenant and adapting to the pagan life around them. As late as the final years of the first Jewish State, about 2,500 years ago, Jeremiah is revolted to find the savage cult of Moloch, the sacrifice of children by fire, still practiced by Jerusalemites in the valley of Ben Hinom outside the Holy City.

Today, we moderns fancy ourselves civilized but the old legend subtly disabuses us of such conceit. It reminds us how we still reject the ethical values of Sinai. "Thou shalt not commit murder"... twentieth-century man has shed more human blood than all his ancestors in the annals of history. "Thou shalt not commit adultery"... a popular sport among us that has reached a new stature of respectability. "Thou shalt not steal"... the old Ishmaelite objection still resonates today: how else can one make a living?

I share the God with every flower, I drink the nectar of the hour ...
Ralph Waldo Emerson

If you were to ask: what is this Sinai covenant all about? I would say: it defines the minimal standards of a civilized human life. Both for the individual and the community, it sets basic norms of humane ethics and spiritual growth. It is in substance a guide to help us emerge out of anachronistic, destructive lifestyles that do violence to our humanity.

To be sure, those who aspire to higher levels of spiritual evolvement will not be content with the minimum; they will go, in the classic talmudic phrase, "beyond the requirements of the law." Everyone, however, can sanctify life by fulfilling the precepts of scripture and become a "co-partner with the Holy One Blessed Be He" in the creation of a renewed society on earth.

There are 613 such precepts in the first five biblical books of the Torah. These include both positive norms, such as "You shall love the stranger for you were strangers in the land of Egypt," and negative norms, such as, "You shall not oppress the widow or orphan.!' They are also divided into ethical norms, those relating people to each other, i.e., "Honor your father and mother," and also spiritual norms, those relating people to God, i.e., "Remember the sabbath to sanctify it."

One of the Bible's surpassing achievements was to reject completely the dualistic view of reality, which separates the religious from the secular, the ideals we profess in sacred places and on sacred days from the values we live by in our real lives at home and in our social world.

Consider this revealing insight from biblical semantics. The Hebrew Scriptures are universally acknowledged as the religious sourcebook for all three major religions in western civilization. Both the New Testament and the Koran validate their doctrine in the covenantal and prophetic tradition of the Old Testament. Yet, there is not a single word in biblical Hebrew that means religious or secular. Modern Hebrew philologists had to create a word to connote the western concept of "religion," so they borrowed a late biblical term, "dat," which really means custom or edict, and converted it to mean religion.

Why is the word religion not to be found in the whole ancestral religious literature of western culture? Because the concept of religion and its antonyn, saecularis, are words and ideas that derive from a dualistic view of reality, a view rejected by the monotheistic world out-look of Hebrew scripture.

You can't achieve a lifestyle of sanctity, according to this view, by withdrawing from the so called secular world and becoming religious. On the contrary, since both the secular and religious are variant elements of one reality, the core of human responsibility is to sanc-tify both. This idea is nowhere better illustrated than in the famous Holiness Code of Leviticus.

"And the Eternal spoke to Moses saying: speak to the whole community of Israel and tell them. . .

'You shall be holy for I, the Eternal your God am holy. You shall revere everyone, your mother and father and keep my sabbaths. . . and when you reap the harvest of your land, you shall leave the corner of the field. You shall not take the glean-ing of your harvest (the grain that falls to the ground when the reaper cuts) nor shall you glean your vineyards nor take for yourself the fallen fruit of your garden. You shall leave them for the poor and the stranger. . . You shall not steal nor deal falsely nor lie to one another. . . You shall not delay the pay-ment of a worker's wages overnight. . . You shall not gossip or slander nor stand by idly when the blood of human being is spilled. . . You shall not hate any person in your heart. . . You shall not take vengeance nor bear a grudge but you shall love your neighbor as yourself. . . If a stranger live among you, you shall not exploit him; he is to be treated like the native citizen among you and you shall love him as yourself for you were strangers in the land of Egypt; I am the Eternal God.' "

Here the essence of Torah guidance is captured. All life on earth needs to be sanctified, that is to say, el-evated to higher forms of ethical and spiritual fulfill-ment. In your personal, family, or communal life, at home or at business, on the farm or in the city, nationally and internationally, new opportunities are always open to

29

you for ethical growth and spiritual enrichment. An ancient Hebrew prayer in the morning and afternoon liturgy of daily, sabbath and festival worship epitomizes that theme: "We will sanctify Your Divine Essence on earth even as it is hallowed on high."

Preeminent as a gage of biblical ethics, are the laws concerning the treatment of strangers. Of all the social diseases inherited from prehistoric times, the one that has afflicted humanity most catastrophically is the universal malaise of xenophobia, the fear and hatred of strangers. In the ancient world, if you were not a member of a tribal in-group, you had no claim to the humane treatment reserved for its members. Even the highly developed Greek civilization referred to the non-Greek as, barbar, a barbarian, not entitled to the protection of just laws applicable only to native Hellenes. History knows no plague more deadly than xenophobia in decimating society with racial, religious and national suffering, persecution and war. In our society, it persists, as a primary catalyst for thermonuclear extinction.

Literatures of many ancient middle eastern cultures have been unearthed during the archeological revolution of the past century. To date, the only one among them to confront this xenophobic threat and to legislate extensively against it is the Hebrew Bible. Unprecedented when they first appeared 33 centuries ago, there are 26 positive and negative statutes in the Pentateuch that define ethical relations with the stranger: One system of law applies equally to Jew and non-Jew alike. Strangers are under the same legal protection as Jews against the practice of oppression, exploitation, or the ravages of poverty. They are also entitled to the same considerations of compassion, charity, and love. With a singular sensitivity to the feelings of the minority outsider, unparalleled in any legislative system down to the modern age, the Bible ordains: "You shall not take advantage of the stranger; you know the stranger's heart for you were once strangers enslaved in the land of Egypt."

The claim is by no means made here that ethical achievement in ancient literature was limited to Hebrew Scripture. On the contrary, the literatures of the ancient Tigris-Euphrates cultures, such as Sumer, Accad, Chaldea, Babylon, Assyria, and Mesopotamia, as well as that of the Nile civilization, evidence great ethical progress. What shall we say of the profound and lasting contributions to ethics by the Greeks and Romans?

Two assertions are, however, advanced here. One is that in Hebraic scripture we find the definitive effort to unite the ethical and spiritual. This idea is so commonplace today that we assume it must always have been so. It wasn't.

Among the great semitic cultures contemporary with and precedent to the ancient Hebrews, ethical concern was largely a secular, state affair. The great Hammurabi Code of ancient Babylon and its predecessors, the laws of King Lipit Ishtar and King Ur Nammu, all of which anteceded the laws of Exodus, served as the legal system of Babylonian and Sumerian society. The gods of Babylon (more than 700 are listed in the Tell El Farah tablets c. 2700 B.C.E.) were not overly concerned with ethical interrelationships between mere men. Human beings were vassals of the gods; their raison d'etre was to please their divine masters.

Plato and Aristotle wrote immortal works on ethics. They remain classics of moral philosophy embarrassingly irrelevant to Greek religion. The gods of Olympus were completely amoral; by the most primitive ethical standards, to say nothing of Aristotelian ence

31

standards, they might be judged immoral. Greek mythology portrays the gods lying, stealing, raping, and murdering with no apologies or guilt. The fact is that these ancient gods cannot be judged ethically because they were above the law. Ethics was the concern of mere mortals. The immortal gods transcended moral law as absolute sovereigns transcended their subjects.

One and a half thousand years before Aristotle, the founder of the Jewish people and faith, Abraham,is described as entering into a remarkable dialogue with God. Abraham is informed that the cities of Sodom and Gomorrah by the Dead Sea would be wiped out because of their violence and crime. He can't believe it and, with a great chutzpah (loosely translated as colossal nerve), appropriate to the first Jew, he argues effectively with God. Maybe there are 50 decent people in Sodom... how can You destroy them indiscriminately with the evildoers? In an immortal phrase that heralds the marriage of ethics to religion, Abraham challenges the Lord Himself: "Will the God of the entire world Himself do an injustice?" God says in effect: you're right, Abe, if Sodom has 50 good people, I'll spare the town. But Abraham's a Jew. He bargains further: maybe there are only 45, 40, 30, 20 even 10 good people? God gives in.

Abraham had somehow advanced beyond the distant, capricious, amoral gods of antiquity. In him, the first stirrings of an ethical monotheism were bringing into focus a new covenantal vision of the relationship between human beings and their Creator. Its passion gave birth, at Sinai, to a covenant people and changed the course of human civilization. Ethics and religion were now united for better or worse.

The second claim advanced here is that much of the ethical sensitivity of scripture, and also a great many of its spiritual teachings, reflect the traumatic experi-

32

of the Jews in Egyptian slavery. All manner of human exploitation, oppression, and degradation, which had been endured for centuries in Egypt, were now expressly prohibited in biblical law. An overwhelming passion for justice, a compelling concern for the weak, the helpless, the poor and the underdog were ethical reactions to the bitter memories of the past.

America's 20th century master of biblical archeology, William Foxwell Albright, characterized the religious status quo of Moses' youth in Egypt as "singularly repulsive." It was a composite of Canaanite cults featuring ritual prostitution of both sexes, heterosexual and homosexual, snake worship and human sacrifice, together with native Egyptian traditions of animal worship and an almost morbid societal preoccupation with death and elaborate funerary practices. "Small wonder, that the new (Mosaic) faith reacted intensely against all kinds of sacred prostitution and human sacrifice, against magic and divination and against funerary rites and the cult of the dead."

There is no question that the "remembrance of the liberation from Egypt" left an indelible impress upon all subsequent biblical ethics and spiritual growth. The phrase itself became a refrain, its trauma seared into the deep subconscious of folk memory for all time.

Water flows over these hands.
May I use them skillfully to preserve our precious planet.
Thich Nhat Hanh

Waking up this morning, I smile.
Twenty-four brand new hours are before me.
I vow to live fully in each moment
and to look at all beings with eyes of compassion.
Thich Nhat Hahn

3. *Appreciating and Enjoying Life*

To sanctify life on earth by performing the sacred commandments is the thrust of the Covenant...not out of fear or guilt or mechanical obedience but in joy and love. "Serve the Eternal with joy," sings the poet of Psalms. This service of joy is a major Biblical refrain. "Rejoice in your festival." "Be happy in all the goodness which the Lord, your God, has bestowed upon you." For Isaiah, joy is the way to relate to God..." You shall rejoice in the Eternal and glory in the Holy One of Israel." In his view, the sabbath was not to be observed, as a depressing killjoy but "you shall declare the sabbath a delight."

That concept grew into a classic expression of authentic Biblical lifestyle, "simchah shel mitzvah" (the joy derived from doing good deeds). A talmudic teaching suggests that "the Divine Presence, the Shekhinah of God, does not abide among the gloomy but among those who fulfill His will in joy."

A joyous sanctification of life leads us to the way of harmony, balance and integration. Neither the extremes of celibacy nor of orgiastic sexual excess (both widely practiced in ancient Canaanite and Hellenistic religion) but a happy marriage of consecration is the path of divine service. Marriage is the first precept in scripture; it is called kiddushin, sanctification, in Hebrew. The Talmud taught: "A man who lives without a wife, lives

35

without joy, without blessing, without Torah and without fulfillment."

"Wine makes the heart glad," wrote the psalmist. There's no sanctity in denying yourself its joy nor in abusing it to stupefy the senses; both extremes were, in fact, espoused by ancient religious cults. The way of Torah is to recite the blessing of kiddush, sanctification over the wine, expressing appreciation to God for the fruit of the vine and enjoying it with a balanced moderation.

We touch here the inner heart of the scriptural style. Its goal is to sensitize us to new options every day for consecrating our world in loving joy.

The midrash observes: "An insensitive man is dead even while he lives. For he looks upon the glorious sunrise and has no praise for Him 'Who creates light' and sees the splendid sunset but has no blessing for Him 'Who brings on the evening twilight'. He also eats and drinks but never utters a word of thanks to his Provider. Those who have evolved to righteousness will bless God for all the food and drink they enjoy and for all the sights and sounds they experience."

Children of the covenant will consecrate every sensate experience they enjoy with a brakhah, a blessing of praise to God. There are specific blessings for the enjoyment of bread, wine, fruits of the tree and produce of the ground, general foods and drink. . .for the joy of new clothing, fragrances, new possessions and experiences, the sight of natural beauty, radiant sky, stars, sun and moon, majestic mountains, seas, deserts, rain, thunder, lightning, rainbows,trees, plants, flowers, animals, birds, creatures of the sea, handsome men, and beautiful women (and who is not?). One sage suggested that a sensitive person could find 100 occasions every day for blessings of appreciation.

What are we dealing with here, the old-time cliche of thanksgiving? I draw your attention to a masterful poem in the Hebrew liturgy of all three daily worship services:

"We thank You, Our God and God of our fathers. . .
for our lives committed to Your hand
and our souls entrusted to You,
and for your miracles and wonders
within us and around us every day —
evening, morn, and noon."

Children look for supernatural miracles. An adult stands in awe before the infinite miracles of everyday reality. Who can confront the unfathomable space, mass and motion of our universe without radical amazement? How can we open our eyes and see, taste, smell, hear and feel all the wondrous beauty of this world without profound appreciation? How much awareness do we need to marvel at the miracles of our own body, with its trillions of cells each performing a hundred intricate biochemical tasks to keep us alive, and all of it independent of our conscious knowledge or will?

The point is that sensitivity to the preciousness of life involves far more than an annual ritual of thanksgiving. Here again our understanding is deepened by Hebrew semantics. The word khol, which is the antonym for sacred (kadosh), actually means more than profane. It derives from a root meaning empty, commonplace, insignificant. What is affirmed philologically is that to sanctify life is to assign it supreme value and, therefore, to preserve and enhance it.

On the other hand, to be unappreciative of life is to contribute directly to its trivialization and ultimately to its destruction. Our century more than any before it has validated that truth. As we began to denude life of sanctity and to render it increasingly void of intrinsic value, we set in motion huge forces of personal, social and ecological devastation, which threaten to annihilate all life together with its support systems on our planet.

If we regard a human being as nothing more than a descendant of one branch of the ape family that made good, if his value does not exceed the total cost of his body's chemical components (we dare not forget that the Nazi masters of the concentration camps manufactured soap out of the body fat of their mass murdered victims), then neither joy, nor love, nor life itself is possible but only expanding hopelessness, anomie, violence and death.

In his final words to the Jewish people, the master teacher of antiquity, Moses laid out the ultimate human options in strikingly modern terms. Unlimited blessings of abundance and joy would be the consequence of sanctifying life. Otherwise, the most tragic maledictions of famine, disease, violence, terror, war, enslavement and holocaust would prevail. None of those disasters has escaped our society, even one which must have seemed improbable more than 3,000 years ago: "The heavens above your head will be as copper and the earth beneath you as iron. Dust and ashes will rain upon your land; it will fall down upon you from the sky until you are utterly demolished."

We are well advanced today in the insane pursuit of anti-life options...the pollution of human bodies by congeries of life dissipating drugs and chemicals... the pitiless ravaging of our atmosphere, rivers, oceans, forests, mountains, deserts, fields and cities, befouling our air, poisoning our food and water...the erosion of our social institutions and communities in accelerating violence, terror and genocide.

Never before did any generation need more desperately to rechannel itself. Our survival depends upon our capacity to achieve a new commitment to life, to its sanctification, celebration, and ennoblement. That life affirming commitment is what scripture demands most, that we become more aware of the wondrous gift of life and perform those sacred deeds which can renew our personal, social and natural ecologies.

An ancient midrash (oral transmission of tradition) sums it all up. "When the Holy One Blessed Be He created Adam, He took him on a tour of all the trees in Eden and said to him: 'Observe carefully how precious and beautiful all my creations are. I fashioned everything for your enjoyment, make sure you never despoil or destroy my planet for if you do, no one will repair it after you!"

If we raise our children so they are orphaned from nature, unable to feel comfortable and live in productive harmony with nature, then they will be at the mercy of technology.

But if we can give them a reverence for the earth and a confidence in their ability to live in productive harmony with nature, then technology will fit easily into a total, inter-related approach to life.

James Hubbell

4. A Lifetime of
Spiritual Democracy

t boggles the mind to confront the truth that so modern a concept as spiritual democracy was conceived and implemented in a social experiment more than 3,000 years ago. Yet, that is precisely what is recorded at Mt. Sinai. The biblical covenant provided a constitutional guide for the development of a community in which all would share in an equality of sacred status and reponsibility; and all would be challenged to realize their spiritual, intellectual, and ethical potentialities. This was spelled out explicitly for the generation who stood with Moses to receive the Torah. They were told that, if they lived by its teachings, they would become a people of treasured nobility: "and you will be unto Me a nation of priests and a sacred people."

If among other cultures, sanctity had been monopolized by the professional clergy, here it was to be opened to the whole community. To this day, there is neither clergy nor laity in Judaism; nobody possesses theurgic powers or special relationships to God that are not equally enjoyed by all the others. The semantics of classical Hebrew know no term meaning clergy or laity because the concept itself is incompatible with the goals and spirit of religious democracy. The rabbi is not and has never been a clergyman; he is a teacher of Torah and his congregation are not laymen but students. A gifted modern scholar of Torah observed: "Ten Jews are required for the minyan, (a quorum for public worship in Judaism) nine rabbis are not enough!"

"You are all children of the Lord, your God", scripture tells us in Deuteronomy. We are dealing here not simply with spiritual rights and privileges but also with equal responsibilities and opportunities for a life of sanctification. That represented something new in the world. Every religion had its saints and mystics. Here was an experiment in what Max Kadushin calls "normal mysticism," in which every person was encouraged to draw close to the Shekhinah, the Divine Presence, each according to his or her capacity and inner time table of self evolvement. The key to it all was to be a joyful performance of the mitzvah, the deed that sanctifies everyday life.

A charming "midrashic agada" sheds light upon the efficacy of the loving mitzvah. The story is told of Rabbi Simeon ben Shetah that he bought a donkey from an Arab. His disciples discovered a precious stone hidden around the neck of the animal. They rushed to their teacher and said:

~ Rabbi, God's blessing bestows wealth.

And Simeon ben Shetah answered his students:

~ I purchased the donkey not the gem.

And he went and returned the jewel to the Arab, who proclaimed:

~ Blessed be the Lord, God of Simeon ben Shetah.

This experiment in spiritual democracy, in motivating people to achieve higher levels of ethical, spiritual, and intellectual fulfillment, was not confined to the Jewish community. The loving performance of a mitzvah reaches out for a response in the hearts of all people. It

41

can build bridges of understanding, empathy, affection, and peace.

Tradition is explicit in this matter. You don't have to be Jewish to inform your life with Torah. Rabbi Meir taught: "A non-Jew who occupies himself with Torah study and practice is equal in status to the High Priest. How do we know this? It is written in Scripture: 'You shall keep My statutes and judgments which give life to the person who fulfills them.' The Torah doesn't say to the Priest, Levite, or Israelite who fulfills them but to every person (Jew or non-Jew) who fulfills them."

I would like to register, in this regard, a personal observation. Through all of my adult life in Torah study, I have been turned on to the largesse of spirit that animates this and another cognate teaching of the Talmud: "The righteous among all peoples of the world have their portion in eternal salvation." I consider this authoritative doctrine in Jewish law a crowning achievement and historical breakthrough in the development of spiritual democracy. Some 18 centuries ago, the Jewish tradition advanced the idea that people need not disown their own native religious heritage in order to achieve salvation, that all persons of whatever faith or no faith, who live ethically and practice justice and compassion, are eligible for eternal redemption.

That stands out in bold relief against the claim of many sectarian religions even in modern times that there is no salvation outside their church, a claim beset with two disturbing problems. The first is a problem of spiritual imperialism which arrogates for itself an exclusive monopoly on eternal redemption and finds it necessary, therefore, to maintain a worldwide effort to wean people away from their ancestral traditions. The second is an incredible, moral denigration of the God concept inherent in such ecclesiastical imperialism. How can a compassionate Creator deny salvation to any of His children on grounds of accidental birth into a particular community? Not religious imperialism but only thorough going spirtual democracy is compatible logically and ethically with faith in a merciful God.

The essence of the *intent* in major religions appears to be the same, although they are verbalized differently.

THE GOLDEN RULE

Judaism: *What is hateful to you, do not to your fellowmen. That is the entire Law; all the rest is commentary.*
Talmud Shabbat, 31a

Christianity: *All things whatsoever ye would that men should do to you, do ye even so to them: for this is the Law and the Prophets.* Matthew, 7, 12

Brahmanism: *This is the sum of duty: Do naught unto others which would cause you pain if done to you.*
Mahabharata, 5, 1517

Confucianism: *Surely it is the maxim of loving kindness: Do not unto others that you would not have them unto you.*
Analects, 15, 23

Taoism: *Regard your neighbor's gain as your own gain, and your neighbor's loss as your own loss.*
T'ai Shang Kan Ying P'ien.

Zoroastrianism: *That nature alone is good which refrains from doing unto another whatsoever is not good for itself.*
Dadistan-i-dinik, 94, 5

Islám: *No one of you is a believer until he desires for his brother that which he desires for himself.* Sunnah

5. A Lifestyle of Learning

O f all the mitzvot, one is paramount: the study of Torah. Why its preeminence? "When the sages gathered at Lydda, the question was raised: what is more important, Torah study or practice? Rabbi Tarfon said: practice. Rabbi Akiba countered: study. And the assembly of scholars decided that study is more important since it leads to practice."

Of all the instruments for sanctifying and ennobling life, learning is the most powerful. What in a human being reflects the divine essence more directly than the mind? To cultivate it in study brings us closest to our Creator.

Nothing in the experimental blueprint of the Covenant was more nobly conceived than this sacred effort to form a community of learning. It was altogether a new phenomenon on earth. Education confers power; it was, therefore, guarded jealously by the ruling classes of antiquity, the priests and royalty. But Israel was covenanted to become "a nation of priests and holy people." It followed then that learning must become the sacred privilege and primary obligation of all.

The implementation of that idea opened a new chapter in the history of education. As early as the first century, free and universal elementary education for boys, starting at the age of six, was instituted in the districts and cities of the second Jewish state. It remained unique until the birth of the American free public school system in the nineteenth century.

Adult education on a communal basis had its origin

about 2,400 years ago in the early days of the second Jewish state, with the introduction by Ezra of a synagogue tradition mandating Torah readings and popular instruction on sabbaths and festivals, as well as Mondays and Thursdays every week. Moreover, synagogues in all the cities and towns of Israel offered daily opportunity for adult learning in their Bet Ha-Midrash, (House of Study). More intensive facilities for academic scholarship were available at the Yeshivot academies; they were open to all without regard to social or financial status.

It was, however, the Jewish community of Babylon during the fourth century that developed the first nationwide system of non-academic adult education. Known as the Kallah, it was organized on a bisemester basis. Twice a year, during the months of Adar (before Passover) and Elul (before the New Year), representatives from all Jewish communities throughout the vast Persian Empire would gather at the central academies to review with its leading scholars the curricular program of the past semester and to plan study programs for the new term. Not untill 1,500 years later did the first systematic, non-academic education of adults appear in the West, with the first Scandinavian experiments in residential high schools and colleges, the British workers' classes and the American classes for immigrants during the nineteenth century.

Maimonides, the greatest master of Jewish law and philosophy in the middle ages, records this talmudic law in his famous code, The Mishneh Torah: "Every Jewish person is enjoined to study Torah. How long does this mandate apply? Till the day of death." For more than two millennia, the life of learning has been for the Jewish people the embodiment of their highest sancta.

"Torah learning is of a greater eminence than royalty or priesthood." Other religious traditions have enshrined simple faith, even irrational faith, above knowledge and learning. Tertullian's credo is the classic example. "Credo quia absurdum est" — (I believe even if it be absurd) By contrast, Hillel taught several centuries before Tertullian: "Ignorance is incompatible with sanctity." Why? Because ignorance is both sterile and corrosive; sterile, in that it does not permit spiritual growth and corrosive, in that blind faith easily degenerates into unrestrained superstition. It also diminishes the essence of God within each of us and impedes the realization of our potentialities.

We are not accustomed to think of study, as joyful. Education in western society has become increasingly vocational, goal-oriented, and dull. Not so with the study of Torah. In its authentic expression, it was li-shmah, study for its own sake. To be sure, vocational skills were very important and mandated for every person but they were acquired experientially in apprenticeship. Torah learning was what you did for your own personal growth, to cultivate the divine latencies of mind, heart, and soul within you...in short, to become a mensch, a humane person, just, compassionate and empathetic, a worthy heir of the Eternal Covenant and participant in the sacred community of Israel, past, present, and future.

Torah study became the summum bonum of Jewish Life; both what the French call *une affaire de coeur*, a passionate love affair, and also a joyful adventure of the spirit that has endured over many centuries.

The primacy of Torah study undergirded this whole experiment in social democracy and produced an unprecedented society of learning among the people.

The Jewish community expected all its members to learn and reserved its highest social esteem for the learned. More than the wealthy, or the powerful, the

46

talmid haham, the disciple of the wise, the teacher was accorded primary social honor. God Himself is praised as "the Teacher of Torah to His people Israel" and is depicted as lecturing before His heavenly academy. That analogy is no mere poetic metaphor. A well known talmudic teaching requires that "the reverence of your teacher be like your reverence of God." In view of the rapidly degenerating attitude towards teachers in our contemporary school system, where teachers are victimized openly by the contempt, humiliation and even violent attack of their students, this value emphasis becomes even more persuasive.

The ancient sages taught: "A scholar takes precedence over the king of Israel. Why? If the king dies, every Israelite is worthy of royalty. But if a scholar dies, his unique learning is irreplaceable." I am convinced that this overwhelming communal priority, which was assigned to the value of learning and inbred for many centuries, was more potent than any inherited genetic pool in developing the intellectual vigor of the Jewish people to this day. An impressive proof of that vigor is the statistical fact that, although Jews constitute less than one-half percent of the world's population, they have won, nevertheless, more than 20 percent of all Nobel Prizes ever awarded.

The source of this cultural vitality was the elevation of study to the highest spiritual dimension of worship. In verbal prayer, one addresses God; in study, He speaks to us. Of transcendent importance in the biblical experiment of spiritual democracy was the challenge to cultivate in every person the fullest capacity to receive that communication.

The importance of educating one's heart, mind and soul throughout all stages of life cannot be over-emphasized. Rabbi Penner's feelings about education are echoed by many of the world's great thinkers.

The Jewish religion, because it was a literature sustained religion, led to the first efforts to provide elementary education for all the children in the community.   Wells, *Outline of History*

The aim (of Jewish education) is to develop a sincere faith in the holiness of life and a sense of responsibility for enabling the Jewish people to make its contribution to the achievement of the good life.   Kaplan, *Future of the American Jew*

I used to spend whole days without food and whole nights without sleep in order to meditate. But I made no progress. Study, I found, was better. Study without thought is vain; thought without study is perilous.   Confucius

The primary goal of education in a free society is to prepare people to make wise decisions. There are, to be sure, other goals to be achieved to enable this to happen. But ultimately, the goal is education in action -- namely, knowledge and thought translated into wise decisions.

The education that fosters the ability to make wise decisions should be as long as life itself and should take place in many situations...   C. Scott Fletcher, Presiden   *The Fund for Adult Education*

Education is of course learning something. More importantly, it is becoming something... A person is something that it takes time to make; there is on everyone an invisible sign, "Work in Progress;" and the considered effort to get along with the work is education...

The end of man's existence is not cooperation. It is not even safety. It is to live up to the fullest possibilities of humanity. And man is human only as he knows the good and shares that knowing with those to whom he is, in humanity, bound.   Robert Redfield,   *Department of Anthropology , University of Chicago*

6. A Lifestyle of Family Celebration

Never before has the family been more devastated than in our century. Disintegrating rapidly before massive forces of socio-economic pressure, the family is eroding also from within. Notwithstanding all our well publicized advances in social sciences, we cannot begin to cope with the spreading corrosiveness of divorce. We are unable even to contain it at its present rate; everybody knows that next year the statistics will be worse.

Nor have the alternative lifestyles fared any better. If anything, the union of unmarried spouses, heterosexual and homosexual, and all the recent experiments in dyads, triads and variegated communal families are proving less stable than traditional forms. Some of America's most talented, young playwrights are dramatizing these new family relationships in our most arresting current theatre. The patterns of alliance may sound new but the pain of rupture and the loneliness of separation are very old. Margaret Mead observed wryly: "No matter how many communes anybody invents, the family always creeps back."

Does anyone doubt that the accelerating breakup of the family is an explosive time bomb over our society penultimate only to a thermonuclear apocalypse? The latter has an awesome finality about it, an end to all problems and to human life itself; whereas the former consumes us with a wildly contagious epidemic of anti-

49

social violence and crime, anger and alienation, hatred and cruelty. Even more dangerous is our impotence to deal with it.

If we were to ask: what kind of homes do we moderns live in? The agonizing truth is that many of us don't live in homes at all, but in motels we call home. What differentiates a home from a motel? Nothing physical. The acceptable motel in America is furnished with wall-to-wall carpeting, color TV, solid furniture, good kitchen facilities et al. What really distinguishes a home, even a modest home, from a motel, no matter how lavish its decor, is a certain tone, an atmosphere, a spiritual quality, more real than any physical appurtenance.

Motels are suffused with an air of transiency. They provide room for people to sleep, look at TV, eat and run. A sterile boredom pervades the motel and it becomes intolerably stifling after a few days. Yet, that is precisely the kind of place many American families live in today. Some in small apartment motels and others in spacious, estate size motels, but the transient air of sterility is the same. Nothing is happening there – no real communication, no celebration, no sharing, no growing, no commitment. Day follows day routinized and undistinguishable. Why should it surprise us to learn that so many marriages end in sheer boredom? There is no life nourishment in the vacuum of a motel. The enviroment is sterile.

Biblical tradition excels in its perception of the social dynamics relating a family's health to the spiritual-cultural vitality of its home milieu. Other religious groups sought to preserve the family by prohibiting divorce. Not so in scriptural law which grants divorce without difficulty. The historic power of the Jewish family derives not from a negative prohibition against dissolving marriage, but from a positive consecration and creative enrichment of home living.

At the core of this communal experiment in spiritual democracy was the sanctification of the home no less than the sanctuary. Both biblical and post-biblical traditions enriched the home with (to borrow a classic title from William James) varieties of religious experience throughout the calendar year. They bear the stamp of social engineering genius.

Every seventh day, a major happening engages the family at home. As the sun sets on Friday eve, the sabbath is welcomed with great joy. All members of the family have prepared for the celebration and the house sparkles, as befitting a reception of royal guests. In fact, it is a deed of special merit to invite sabbath guests into your home — friends, strangers, the lonely and the needy — to make them feel part of your family and to share your sabbath feast of joy with them. The wife-priestess of her miniature sanctuary kindles the sabbath candles and offers a blessing to illumine her home with the light of Torah. The husband-priest chants the Kiddush, blessings of sanctification over the wine, in which all assembled around the festive table partake joyfully.

The most colorless, drab and motel-like residence can be quickened to life-renewing spirit by an authentic family experience of sabbath tradition. No quick-frozen-TV dinner-and-run routine tonight. This is a family celebration. There are happy songs to be sung, time honored delicacies to be savored, good conversation to be shared, open communication between parents and children to be enjoyed and a cultural-spiritual enrichment to be experienced by all.

Nobody is in a hurry. For one evening in the week,

everyone is free from tyrannical servitude to the stress of time. In a relaxed mood parents ask the children what they learned in school during the past week. An ancient legacy of intuitive wisdom is wrapped up in this custom that confers rich benefits upon the children. It motivates them to review and master the week's lessons in order to discuss them intelligently. But even more significantly, it gets the clear message across to them that their parents really care about their education and that what they do in school is important. For many centuries, Jewish children have been the beneficiaries of this signally effective "head start" in the life of learning.

As to its generic purpose from earliest biblical days, the classic sabbath seeks to refresh and renew the body, mind and soul of every individual celebrant in the family. Its debut almost 4,000 years ago, in an age when the overwhelming masses of human beings toiled in unrelived misery and only priesthood and royalty enjoyed days of rest and recreation, constituted a major social revolution. Today that revolutionary power is not yet spent. We need desparately a day of liberation from enslavement to work and to all the stress inducing pressures of modern society ...a sacred day that gets us to slow down from our frenetic pace of joyless survival...a day for celebration, a day that turns our homes into growth centers for weekly creative encounters in self-realization and family renewal. That day is the Sabbath, which the ancient prophet captured in one felicitous phrase: "You shall call the sabbath a delight."

It became the paradigm for all the biblical festivals, which highlight every season and introduce new modalities of sacred joyful celebration into home life throughout the year.

Passover in the spring is a family festival par excellence; its main event is experienced, not at synagogue, but at home. In a festive atmosphere of family reunion with great love and joy, the Seder Feast of the Passover re-enacts the sacred drama of Israel's ancient struggle for freedom. Its structure recreates in the home an authentic educational milieu and restores to parents their original role, as teachers of their children, a role they fulfilled for thousands of years before our educational system became professionalized. Understood in depth, the Seder Feast is actually an organized lesson plan for a marathon learning experience on the theme of freedom.

Shavuot, the Festival of the Torah Covenant and of the summer's first fruits ~ Succot, the fall harvest festival (biblical ancestor of the American holiday of Thanksgiving) ~ Hannukah, the winter Festival of the Lights and Purim, the merry holiday of winter's end ~ all of them infuse new and happy celebrations in the home with varieties of foods, customs, colors, tones, ideas, music, and discussions. There is a rhythm of peak experiences for the Jewish family in sabbath and festivals rejoicing through all the year's cycle of the weeks, months, and seasons.

Nor was the family lifestyle to be limited to special days. Attention was also given to what the ancient Alexandrian Jewish philosopher, Philo, called "the Festival of Everyday." All the members of the family were encouraged by tradition to invest themselves, their imagination and substance, their learning and love, their time and concern, in enriching their daily home experiences. There is no question but that the home served historically as the fortress of Jewish survival and cultural creativity. It has something vital to say to our age. One more observation. There are fifty chapters in the opening scriptural book of Genesis; thirty-eight of them are filled with stories about family life. Why? The reference

53

is clear. In the social design of creation, family life was assigned a role of indispensable primacy. The ancients felt that human survival and well-being were related directly to the health and strength of the family. Among the valuable insights contained in those last thirty-eight chapters of Genesis, I will comment upon two.

First, the role of women. You have to be impressed with the status and leverage those biblical matriarchs enjoyed almost 4,000 years ago. Abraham, one of history's foremost personalities, father of all three major western religions, is instructed by God: "Whatever Sarah tells you to do, listen to her." And he does!

How many wives today exert that much influence upon the decision making process in their family? One of the constant complaints we all hear from women is that their husbands don't even listen, that their opinions, their feelings, their views are denied the dignity of a hearing. What underscores this old scriptural wisdom on family life is its strong emphasis upon open communications between husband and wife. And even in so male dominated a society as the ancient Near East, the judgments of Sarah, Rebecca, Rachel, Leah, Tamar and others could prevail. The talmud picks up this theme with some good advice to husbands. "If your wife is short, bend down and take her advice."

My second comment focuses upon a simple prose statement in Genesis describing Isaac's marriage to Rebecca. "And Isaac brought her into the tent of his mother, Sarah, and took her for his wife and he loved her." This artful style of simplicity should not divert our attention from an important concept here. We are informed explicitly that Isaac loved Rebecca after their marriage. That runs counter to the prevailing romanticism of our culture. "One should always be in love — that is the reason one should never marry," wrote a modern cynic.

54

Another defined marriage as, "a book of which the preface is written in poetry and the rest in prose." "God," exclaimed a famous Hollywood star, "for two people to live together for the rest of their lives is almost unnatural!"

That puerile romanticism, which confuses puppy dog titillation with love, is the rot that erodes our families and our society. The old biblical idea is much more mature. True love begins with pre-nuptial romance but it doesn't end there; it is renewed and consecrated with marriage. Where husband and wife cultivate their love after the honeymoon enabling it to grow day by day, there is the seed of personal joy, family enrichment and social fulfillment. No substitute has ever been found for a maturing love; it is the quintessence of an enduring family.

Our brief discussion, in this first section, of some Biblical values for a meaningful lifestyle on earth was offered as preparatory guidance and nourishment for you on your journey through the Four Dimensions of Paradise. You will begin in the next section, your first major exploration on this trip, to examine how people communicate with God verbally and non-verbally. How does God speak to human beings? What is the value of such reciprocal communication? How does the Bible serve as a unique intercommunications conduit? And finally how do the Four Dimensions of Paradise provide us with the most comprehensive understanding of Scripture preparing us to enter into that unending cosmic dialogue with God?

Loving earth, work, one another, psyche – all these require unhurried time. Frenzied questing after the icons of modern life (speed, power, instant, more, bigger, unboundedness) devours time and injures the capacity to love. The shy soul is driven inevitably into hiding where she weeps and yearns for a time when men had time to love. The failure to find time for soul is the essential tragedy of our time.

Russell Lockhart, Ph.D.
from *Eros in Language*

BOOK TWO

An Introductory Tour Through The Four Dimensions of Paradise

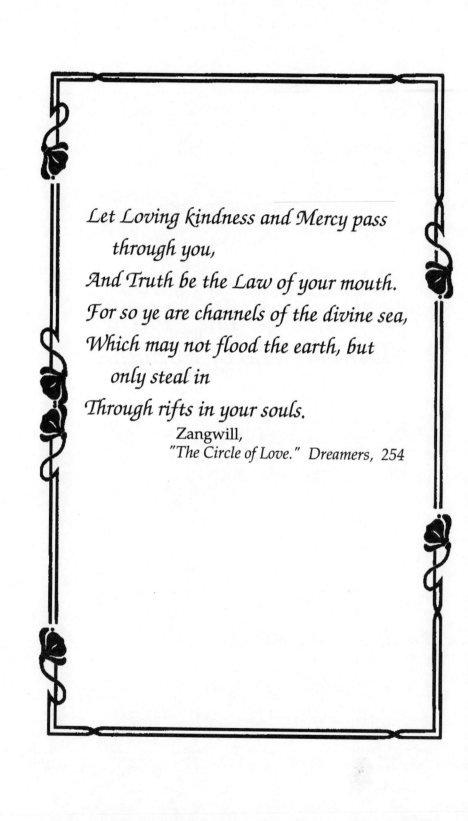

Let Loving kindness and Mercy pass
    through you,
And Truth be the Law of your mouth.
For so ye are channels of the divine sea,
Which may not flood the earth, but
    only steal in
Through rifts in your souls.

Zangwill,
"The Circle of Love." Dreamers, 254

1. Examples of Reciprocal Communications with God

"For Not By Bread Alone Will Humanity Live
But By The Full Yield of God's Word."
Deuteronomy

If happiness could be gained by acquisition, we in America should be the happiest people of all time. Never has any nation been more luxuriantly affluent than ours. There is more acquisitiveness, more "conspicuous consumption" in the United States than anywhere else. We also have the most millionaires here but they don't seem to be happier than others. "Just give me one million bucks," pleaded one of our sharpest wits, "and I'll be delighted to be miserable!"

We were probably the first and possibly the only society to have defined "the pursuit of happiness" as an unalienable human right. And we have been pursuing it eagerly now for 200 years — this American dream of happiness measured by material abundance. Yet gradually we have come to learn that there is no causal connection between joy and accumulation, that happiness is not a packaged thing and that it cannot be quantified.

59

Don't misunderstand me. Material wealth is a great blessing and "poverty diminishes life." But happiness — that is a quality transcending statistics. It requires a sense of meaning to life, the feeling that you and I are something more than a pointless confluence of events, hanging onto a valueless existence and awaiting a useless death. We need to feel that our lives have abiding value, that we are really connected to each other in one human family and that everyone of us is part of a cosmic oneness relating to the creative source of all life and energy.

That need and that feeling is at the heart of all spiritual journeys and all religious movements in all the ages. "My soul yearns for the Lord, my heart and body sing to the Living God," wrote the poet of Psalms. It's a vast, cold and dark universe out there and we all need to draw close to the resplendent light and love of the Eternal. That need was defined by the mystics of Kabbalah as devekut, cleaving to and embracing God.

Wait a minute, you may be protesting. This religious thing is not for me. As a modern, scientific minded rationalist, I don't buy all that spiritual stuff. I can accept the essential unity of the human species and our connectedness with all sentient life, as proposed by Darwinian and post Darwinian biology, and even our relatedness to cosmic matter, as postulated in biochemistry and astrophysics. But God, meaning, value, quality — they don't compute for me.

My friend, your old stable model of science and rationalism is quite passé. The exciting new brain research and avant garde ideas developing in physics, chemistry, biology and mathematics are probing all aspects of reality — qualitative as well as quantitative, causal and synchronous, rational and illusory. Some of these scientific theories are remarkably close to ancient mystical intuitions and biblical ideas. This is not an appropriate

60

time for closing your mind — least of all in science.

The paradigm for our world emerging from today's scientific research is that of a dynamic process of becoming, a radically changing and continuously evolving universe. Impressed by this cosmic image, Buckminster Fuller suggested poetically that we might even perceive of God — as participating in that evolving process:

"Yes, God is a verb, the most active, connoting the vast harmonic reordering of the universe from unleashed chaos of energy." I don't know whether Mr. Fuller is aware of the fact that his idea of God, as an active verb, is precisely the sense of a startling Mosaic conception more than 3,000 years ago. You may remember the story in Exodus, when Moses was commissioned to liberate his people from slavery, he says to God:

~ Here I am going to the children of Israel and I will tell them: the God of your ancestors sent me to you. And they will ask me: what is His name? What shall I answer them? And the Lord said to Moses:

~ Ehyeh Asher Ehyeh.

Which the King James translates incorrectly "I Am that I Am." Since the Hebrew verb Ehyeh is clearly in the future tense, the exact literal meaning for this divine name is *"I Shall Be what I Shall Be."*

All nouns in Hebrew derive from verb roots. But to conceive of God more than 30 centuries ago as rooted in being, as manifest in the divine process of becoming and creating (causing to be), must be considered an intuition of spiritual genius. This biblical choice of the verb to be, as the root meaning of God's name,was expounded by the sages to signify that He was, He is and He will be the Eternal One.

I want to explain, at this point, that the use of the masculine pronoun in reference to God reflects nothing more than our linguistic limitations. In classic Kabbalah, both the masculine and feminine elements are united within the dynamic Godhead, a concept that I share wholeheartedly.

How do we human beings relate to God? That question forms a central theme throughout biblical and Kabbalistic literature. Here we touch briefly upon one aspect of that relationship; a more substantive treatment is in the latter sections of this book.

"And the Lord created humankind in His essence," we are taught by the famous verse of Genesis, according to Maimonides' perceptive interpretation. This teaches us, say the sages, that everyone of us bears a spark of the divine essence, a sacred seed of the Infinite One. And this interrelatedness is, at the same time, intrinsic and reciprocal.

Even as God perpetually creates and renews, so are we constituted to be, not static but expansive, not rigid but open to growth. The Kabbalah goes further. In the universal scheme, God and humanity interact reciprocally complementing, so to speak, and even requiring one another. The Eternal reaches out to us in love, provides for our needs, nourishes, inspires and heals us; we could not survive without His compassion. We in turn can respond to His love by caring for each other, by practicing justice and compassion, by sharing, "as a co-partner with God," in a creative life to fulfill the potentialities of our divine essence.

When we choose that kind of lifestyle in harmony with the divine will, we promote our own healing, diminishing the stress of inner fragmentation, personal alienation and depressive loneliness. We also advance thereby the unity and wholeness of our society. And on a cosmic level, according to Kabbalistic symbology, our input of positive energy helps draw the presence of God closer to us and even to further "the union of the Holy One Blessed Be He and His Shekhinah." In this last symbolism, we find a very bold assertion of human capacity to affect the universal process. Quite obviously here, we have come a long way from our childlike, Sunday school notions about God and ourselves.

The point is that in choosing a life-affirming style, as outlined above, we bring joy to ourselves, contribute to the happiness of others and to the delight of God Himself, as voiced in the cadenced phrase of Psalms, "let the Lord rejoice in His creatures."

Of course, we can pursue anti-life options and, indeed, we seem to be doing so en masse these days. All around us, we see people caught up in compulsive drives to self destruction — not only in the burgeoning sub-cultures of drugs, crime, violence, terrorism, torture, repression, war and genocide but also in more subtle personal propensities for self hatred and death. And all that negative energy cannot be stored away or contained within. It extends outward to accelerate the corrosive disintegration of society and the ultimate annihilation of life. No joy but a pervasive, deepening misery is the consequence of those anti-life styles that violate the conscience of our inner divine essence and the universal laws of our cosmic Creator.

From this perspective, the interrelationship between human beings and God becomes utterly crucial for our survival as well as that of all life systems on earth... and perhaps even beyond. We need, therefore, to examine in the first part of our journey through the Four Dimensions of Paradise the question of how God communicates to us and how we participate in that communications system.

If you had an open line directly to God, what would you say? Tevyeh in Fiddler on the Roof asks Him straight-away why he can't be a rich man...would it upset some divine, cosmic plan if Tevyeh were blessed with wealth? Abraham demanded justice from God. The great Hasidic master, Levi Isaac of Berditchev, summoned God to a court of law to answer the charge: how could He permit so much persecution and suffering to befall His children? An old folk saying has it that if God resided on earth, people would smash His windows.

The age old problem of maintaining a relationship with God, no matter how conceived, in the face of massive evil, savagery and catastrophe all over the world will be confronted in the final section of this book. The story is told of a young Muscovite looking to improve his career who presented himself to the admissions committee of the Soviet Communist Party. He was accompanied by a friend, who waited outside while he entered the hearing for his final interview. The chairman asked him sternly:

~ Do you believe in God?

~ No!

~ What in your opinion should be done with churches, synagogues and mosques in our country?

~ They should all be converted to recreation centers for the workers.

When he came out his friend asked him:

~ How did you do?

~ With God's help, I hope I will pass.

You may be surprised how often and in how many ways you communicate with God verbally and non-verbally; what is more, you may not even be aware of the processes by which He communicates with you.

Surely you can remember peak experiences in your life...when you stood on a mountain ridge enveloped by majestic grandeur...enthralled before a gorgeous lake, a resplendent sunset...entranced under a jeweled sky of stars ineffable. You uttered no word to violate the sacred stillness but your soul vibrated to your Creator its message of ecstatic rapture, thrilled to be alive for this moment of splendor.

Then you came down from the mountain and your soul ecstasy faded under a daily round of problems and tensions.

"Who shall go up to the mountain of God?
And who shall abide in His sacred place?"

The poet knows it's not that difficult to reach the summit; we all do it from time to time. But to stay there, to live an inspired lifestyle of ongoing soul communication with God, even when you are back in the valley of daily affairs, that is the way of authentic spirituality and mysticism. Each of us need to find it for ourselves and your journey through the Four Dimensions of Paradise will help you make your own discovery.

Consider briefly other kinds of non-verbal communication. Growing rapidly of late is the practice of meditation. Whatever the techniques — and they are legion — the common goal is to transcend all the mundane noise, stress and trivial garbage that clog our minds,disable our bodies, enervate our souls and diminish our lives. By reopening quiet lines of communion with cosmic reality, with the infinite source of all energy and harmony, we recharge our batteries, so to speak, and receive rich rewards of healing physically and spiritually.

But you can speak to God in activity, no less than passivity. When you perform a good deed, show compassion and graciousness, extend love, kindness, justice, encouragement, empathy and friendship to another human being, you make a statement that delights your Creator. "All those in whom their fellow humans take delight, the spirit of God delights in them," teach the sages in the Ethics of the Fathers.

But nowhere is divine inspiration communicated more wondrously than in a creative thought. We have not fathomed the mystery of an idea. But if the new holographic theory and its paradigm for the universe and the human mind is valid, we may have in modern biophysics a stunning renewal of some very ancient metaphysical symbolism concerning that mystery. In Kabbalah, we are informed that cosmic emanations of divine light stream continuously upon us all; the comingling of this divine illumination with creative human intelligence (the essence of God in us) generates our ideas, our insights, our intuition and wisdom. In this sense, our personal and collective advance in knowledge, in art, in ethical achievement and in spiritual truth are all the fruit of an eternal dialogue between humanity and God.

If ever you have addressed God verbally it has probably been in prayer. Who doesn't remember the old religious school days, when your creative kindergarten teacher asked you to compose a prayer of your own and you achieved immortality with something like, "Dear God — please put all the vitamins in ice cream and all the minerals in chocolate and send me a lot of both. Amen."

The word prayer, deriving from the Latin precor, means to beseech, to ask for divine favors. You probably know many people as I do, who were turned off all their lives because of the crude abuses of prayer. And that too has a long history. More than 2,500 years ago, Isalah told his generation about this divine response to their unworthy prayers:

"When you lift up your hands,
I will turn away from you —
Even if you utter many prayers, I won't listen.
Your hands are filled with blood.
Wash yourselves clean,
Remove your corrupt deeds from My presence,
Stop doing harm.
Learn to do good. Seek justice.

66

To the oppressed bring relief —
And defend the orphan, the widow in compassion.
Come let us reason together, saith the Lord..."

No real communication with God is possible before cleansing yourself of cruelty, injustice or deceit. And prayer (beseeching) is surely not the only form of worship. Ancient Hebraic tradition includes others: tehilah (the worship of praise) and of bracha (blessing);todah (the worship of thanksgiving) and tefilah (that of awe and self-evaluation).

"Never let your worship become a mere mechanical recitation of words," taught some ancient sages.

How? By searching for new inspiration and creative insight . . .in your worship; otherwise, it becomes meaningless, a burdensome experience. And that has been the fate of too much public worship: dull, mechanical and worse — a performance played by professional clergy to an audience of spectators. Inexorably our age of spectatorship gave birth to the camp of Drive-In services and the hype of televised prayer shows.

Authentic worship cannot traduce you to a passive spectator or an electronic robot viewer. Its purpose is to activate your line of direct communion with God. When that happens, you experience one of the soul searing moments of your life. But it requires some spiritual preparation.

You need to cultivate what the sages call kavanah — (the intent of your heart) a capacity to concentrate your whole being. That is why the ancients preferred to meditate silently and center themselves before communicating with God. Such worship is light years distant from today's widespread boredom. Its hallmark is hitlahavut (a passionate feeling of love and joy); and its goal: hishtalmut — (a new step forward on your path to achieving wholeness, inner harmony and integral balance).

67

In a broad sense, the whole legacy of human civilization records our communication with God. All its positive achievements were inspired by an authentic understanding and creative implementation of that dialogue. Conversely, all its destructive regressions derived from a distortion and violation of that same cosmic interchange.

What had been implicit from the origin of our species became explicit in the Bible and the vast post biblical literature it generated. Here is an uninterrupted heritage of 4,000 years, universally recognized as sacred literature. Recording originally the communication between one people and its Creator, the Bible was gradually adopted by many people as a paradigm for the human divine dialogue.

The biblical energy thus amassed over four millennia has reached a spiritual megapower without analogue in history. The most evolved mystics, the most enlightened spiritual teachers, will authenticate their visions and assess their wisdom within the biblical context.

One of the enduring contributions of these Four Dimensions was to systematize and map out the four major realms of biblical understanding, so that you and I and all of God's children — not just the mystics and scholars — could have a key to enter directly into this system of communication with God from time immemorial. That has been the biblical purpose from the beginning: to cultivate the growth of every human being.

In the next stage of your journey through the Four Dimensions of Paradise, you will explore how the system came to be, what it means, why it is so indispensably significant and how you can share in its divine treasures of wisdom. In these Four Dimensions of Paradise, the intent of that classic scriptural verse is thoroughly realized: "For not by bread alone will humanity live but by the full yield of God's word."

2. The Four Dimensions of Pardes: Their Origin, Interpretation and Implication

פרדס

We are not concerned here with one of the grand conceits of theology: demonstrating proofs for the divine inspiration of Scripture. The believer requires none; the sceptic is likely to deny validity to the entire question; as for the rest, I suspect most couldn't care less.

What all can share is the incontestable truth that more than twenty centuries of recorded experience in every part of our planet testify to the Bible's unique and universal influence upon the flow of human civilization. The master anthropologist, Sir James Gregory Frazer, summed it up well: "Apart from all questions of religious and historical import, the Bible is the epic of the world. All life's fever is there, its hopes and joys, its suffering and sin and sorrow."

His contemporary, the celebrated biologist and savant Thomas Henry Huxley, added: "Throughout the history of the western world, the Scriptures have been the great instigators of revolt against the worst forms of clerical and political despotism. The Bible has been the Magna Carta of the poor and of the oppressed; down to modern times no State has had a constitution in which the interests of the people are so largely taken into account, in which the duties so much more than the privileges of rulers are insisted upon, as that drawn up for Israel in Deuteronomy and in Leviticus; nowhere is the fundamental truth that the welfare of the State, in the long run, depends on the uprightness of the citizen so strongly laid down.The bible is the most democratic book in the world."

Enough commercials! One can, of course, marshall an impressive array of counter opinion in this matter. Even the devil, we are reminded, loves to quote Scripture and I am not sure whether that investment in subverting the Bible may not be taken as a shrewd adversary's tribute, however unintended, to the real power of its influence.

For us the biblical assumption of divine inspiration is, contrary to popular misconception, not the end but the beginning of the problem. Can a literature, no matter how sacred its claims, serve as a conduit for divine communication? What is the nature of such communication? Is it open to everybody or limited to a favored elite? How is the message received? Is it monolithically fixed and immutable or can it be illumined with new interpretations that speak to an ever changing world? If the latter, what then are the parameters or guidelines for such interpretive renewal?

We would be mistaken to think of these questions as the unique probings of the modern mind; they were confronted by the ancients also. Consider this anomaly. On the one hand, Scripture presents an infinitely transcendent God, omniscient beyond our capacity ever to conceive. "As the heavens tower far above the earth... so do My thoughts transcend your thoughts."

On the other hand, every biblical page is filled with the words of an imminent God communicating freely with humans. "And the Lord said to Abraham"; "and the Lord called to Moses and spoke to him." He talks to Jews and non-Jews, to kings, prophets, sages and plain people alike. He communicates directly and indirectly through dreams, visions and parables. His wisdom is bestowed generously and generically in every area of human life, from religion, ethics, politics, law, medicine, nutrition and agriculture to commerce and art. In this last category of art, parenthetically, our perception of the creative process is enriched deeply by a simple, yet striking, biblical phrase that regards art and handcraft as a "wisdom of the heart."

Overwhelmingly this divine communication is conducted through the medium of the word — of all things, the most non-material, imprecise and mystical. What essentially are words, if not the symbols that reflect our sensory experience of reality? And every child knows how very limited our human senses are. Yet, if the Universal Creator chooses to communicate with us, He must refract, as it were, the light of His infinite wisdom through the prism of human language, however constricted and imperfect. Otherwise we could not receive the message.

Two contemporary giants of ancient scriptural learning, the tannaitic masters Akiba and Ishmael differed procedurally on interpreting the biblical word. Rabbi Akiba took the position that the divine communication of scripture is precise, allowing for no superfluous word or phrase. From that premise, he and his disciples proceeded to search for special meaning in those texts that indicated any apparent superfluity or repetition. Rabbi Ishmael, on the other hand, adopted this widely quoted principle: "The Bible speaks in the language of the people." Therefore it is not necessary to deduce specific interpretations from every seemingly excessive word. This dialogue between the two masters and their students illumines many discussions of law and lore throughout classic, post-biblical literature.

I have admired over the years that bold, avant garde view of divine inspiration communicated in popular idiom. One sage is even quoted as suggesting that scripture sometimes exercises the license of hyperbole, to teach by exaggeration...quite a radical view for the third century! When you think of it, this concept of God communicating to us through the limited word symbols of human language has some fascinating implications. First and foremost is this: we need to clarify and interpret what is often linguistically obscure. And if that presents us with a formidable challenge, does it not also offer a human role of dignity — to participate creatively in a reciprocal intercommunication with God?

That challenge was taken seriously in post-biblical Hebrew learning and spawned vast interpretive literatures of prime quality. Among them are the midrashic collections, the talmudic and post-talmudic classics and the theosophic works of Kabbalistic mysticism, which constitute the mainstream of Hebrew learning to this day.

"Rabbi Judah taught in the name of Rab: When Moses ascended on high to receive the Torah, he found the Holy One Blessed Be He tying crowns over the letters. He said:

~ Master of the Universe, for whom are You doing this? And God answered:

~ After many generations, a man will appear by the name of Akiba ben Joseph and he will interpret whole stacks of new laws on each jot and title.

Then Moses asked:

~ Sovereign of the Universe, show him to me.

And God said:

~ Turn around.

And Moses went and sat down at the end of the eighth row in the Academy but he didn't follow the discussion. He felt weak. When Akiba reached a certain point, his students asked:

~ Rabbi, where is the authority for this law? And he answered them:

It is necessary to study the evolution of intuition and reason as revealed humanistically in the evolution of our perception of ourselves.
Jonas Salk

72

~ It is a tradition from Moses at Sinai.

Moses' mind was put at ease. He went back to the Holy One Blessed Be He and asked:

~ Eternal God, You have a man like that and choose to give the Torah through me? And He answered:

~ Be still, That is My decision."

This revealing agadic story opens us to the vast, multicolored world of the Oral Torah. Some fifteen centuries separated Moses from Rabbi Akiba. What had happened in all that time to the Sinaitic Torah? Had it congealed and fossilized like so many other ancient codes and literatures which are unearthed by archaeologists only to be re-entombed among museum antiquities? How, in fact, did it escape that mortal fate?

There is a need for a reconciliation of religion and science, just as it is necessary to reconcile intuition and reason, experience and knowledge. Jonas Salk

A passage in Leviticus lays down the principle that all biblical teachings were given to advance life and the sages reinforced that principle: "to live by these precepts and not to perish by them." In order to sustain life, the Pentateuch, which together with the Prophetic Books and the Later Writings comprise the Written Torah, had to be nourished and renewed by interpretation. That interpretive development was systematized in the Oral Torah, so called because its teachings were handed down by word of mouth from generation to generation before being committed to writing in the second and third centuries.

The need for Midrash, searching out the textual meaning of Written Torah, was built into biblical style itself. The ancients found it, no less than we, to be allusive and cryptically brief, so as to require clarification by the Oral Torah. Moreover, scriptural codes are often generalistic, like the Constitution of the United States, which could never have survived the radical social changes of the last two centuries without a living tradition of interpretive constitutional law, particularized and applied by judicial exposition. Just so did the Oral Torah interpret

73

and apply the general teachings of Written Scripture to the specifics of life, from Moses to Akiba and thereafter to this day.

Consider, for example, the immortal Ten Commandments, which have become the universal standard of ethical civilization. What tremendous power resonates from those grand generalizations. "Honor your father and your mother..." But how? What does it mean to honor or dishonor one's parents? The talmudic and midrashic literatures of the Oral Torah offer many applied interpretations, out of which I choose this personal favorite: "Abimai, the son of Rabbi Abbahu, taught: One man can regale his father with gourmet stuffed fowl and merit Gehenna, whereas another can bind his father to a millstone and be worthy of Heaven. How? A certain man once served his father stuffed chicken and was asked by him:

~ My son, where did you get these delicious chickens?

~ Old man, old man, why don't you shut up and eat. Even the dogs are quiet when fed. That one merits Gehenna. It is also told of another man who worked at the millstone that, when the king sent his agents out to seize forced laborers, he said to his father:

~ Please father, take my place here at the millstone and I will go to grind for the king. If anybody gets whipped or tortured, let it be me and not you. That man has earned his place in Heaven."

Rare treasures of insight, parables, commentaries, legal expositions, interpretations and applied teachings, such as this, illumine every biblical verse in the Oral Torah. What is meant by the commandments, "You shall not murder", or "You shall not steal?" How do we define the minimal, ethical standards of a sacred lifestyle and what area is left for evolvement beyond that which is merely required? I present two masterpieces of ancient commentative wisdom that address those questions with an astonishing cogency for our modern, public relations dominated and propaganda ridden society. "There are seven kinds of thieves and foremost among them is the one who steals the mind of the people..." "Slander is worse than murder; it kills threefold, destroying the criminal, the receiver and the victim. If one draws the sword to kill another, the victim may plead for mercy and the aggressor be moved to reconsider. But once the arrow of slander has been shot it can not be withdrawn." Our age of mass media has brought into clear focus that deadly connection between xenophobic propaganda and the shedding of human blood.

'Commit no slander ; so that infamy and wickedness may not happen unto thee. For it is said that slander is more grievous than witchcraft.'
Avesta

Several problems are raised by the development of the Oral Torah. Is it to be considered a new dispensation of the divine covenant at Sinai, as Christian theology claims for its testament and as Islam professes for the Koran? Where do the sages derive their authority for interpreting the Bible? Or is this a supreme act of sacrilegious hutzpah for humans to undertake the interpretation of God's word, as the ancient Sadducees and the medieval Karaites felt?

In answer to the first question, the Oral Torah has always been honored in the Hebrew mainstream, not as a new covenant but as a direct out growth of the original Covenant at Sinai. Proceeding from the popular image of the Torah, as a tree of life, the Oral Torah teachings were the fruit issuing from that tree. Just as the tree is contained organically in all the fruit it bears for all time, so do the seeds of the Written Torah contain all the potential interpretations which are destined to be issued in the Oral Torah.

That is the thrust of a remarkable Midrash: "Rabbi Isaac taught: what the prophets are destined to prophesy in every generation, they received from Mt. Sinai, even as Moses said to Israel: 'And not with you alone do I establish this covenant...but with those who stand

75

among us today before the Lord, our God, and also with those who are not here among us this day.' And not only did the prophets receive their prophecies from Sinai *but also the sages who are destined to rise up in every generation, every one of them received his teachings from Sinai.* For thus did Moses teach: 'These words the Lord spoke to your congregation (the Congregation of Israel in all ages) on the mountain (of Sinai). . .in a powerful voice adding nothing more.' Rabbi Isaac interprets God's powerful voice at Sinai adding nothing more to mean that all future interpretations were latent in and destined to emerge from that one powerful revelation. To borrow a phrase from contemporary astrophysics, you might call this a "Big Bang" theory of revelation.

If you feel the analogy somewhat forced or cavalier, or both, please note the conclusion of that same midrashic discussion. Rabbi Yohanan asserts that the powerful voice of God at Sinai divided itself into 70 languages to transmit the teachings of Torah in a multilingual message to all humankind. His colleague Rabbi Joshua ben Levi supports that opinion by the analogy of a blacksmith who strikes a mighty blow on his anvil causing many sparks to fly out in all directions. Big Bang theory indeed!

You might be interested, parenthetically, in this latest count. As of February 11, 1981, the complete Bible was available in 275 languages and at least one scriptural book has been published in 1,710 languages. And yet, notwithstanding this unequaled availability of the biblical word, our world seems no more decent or humane for it. I suppose one can say no in 275 or even 1,710 languages. Obviously the divine communication of Scripture needs something more than translation. It needs to be understood and implemented. And that is a primary goal of the Four Dimensions of Paradise.

Engaging though it be, we leave this parenthesis and

return to the heart of our midrash. What it does is nothing less than to validate the authority of the whole Oral Torah tradition and its organic growth from Sinaitic origins to "the end of days." The sages were not timid about asserting that authority; it was for them a clear biblical mandate. If a criminal or civil case be too difficult for you to determine ...you shall come...to the judge of those days to enquire and be given the decision of judgment. And you shall carry out that decision...According to the Torah which they shall teach, so shall you do...and not turn away from it to the right or the left." To expound, adjudicate and apply the Bible was a sacred responsibility, from which there could be no retreat.

One of the most gutsy stories in all of religious literature illustrates the spiritual courage of these Oral Torah scholars. During an intense discussion at the Central Academy almost 1,900 years ago, the Talmud records that Rabbi Eliezer differed with the majority opinion of his colleagues. "Let heaven prove that my opinion is the valid law," he said. Whereupon a heavenly voice went forth and announced: "The law follows Rabbi Eliezer on all matters." Then Rabbi Joshua arose and stated: "Scripture itself tells us: 'This Torah is not in the heavens.' We cannot, therefore, decide by heavenly voice for the Lord already has written in His Torah at Sinai: 'You shall follow the majority decision.' Some time afterward, Rabbi Nathan encountered Elijah the Prophet and asked him: "What did the Holy One Blessed Be He do at that moment?" And Elijah answered: "He smiled and said: 'My sons prevailed over Me, My sons prevailed over Me."

Here is admittedly a strong specimen of the compelling commitment those sages of Oral Torah felt to the enhancement of human dignity and nobility. That commitment was not new but rather a renewal of core

ideas from every section of the Written Bible. To participate in the divine communication of Scripture involves
a very special kind of responsibility.

"Were the Bible given cut and dried," taught the sage,
Rabbi Jannai, "no space would have been allowed for
human participation." The Creator, however, preferred
to communicate in a Bible that is not sealed or immutable
but open and evolving. His delight apparently is to encourage His children, who share in the infinity of His
intelligence, to become active participants with Him in a
communicative process of ongoing scriptural study.

The relationship imaged here is not that of a tyrannical
master placing his commands on his mute, golem like
slave, but rather like a loving father who speaks tenderly
to his child and rejoices to receive a wise response. Another favorite metaphor of rabbinic literature is that of
God, as the Teacher par excellence, who instructs His
students in Torah with great compassion and takes much
pleasure in evoking a responsive effort from them signi-
fying their educational growth and maturation. In this
view, the divine inspiration of scripture is not a mono-
logue but a creative dialogue for all to share and, by
learning, probing and growing, fulfill those divine
latencies resident within us individually and socially.

I think it fair to say here that the ideal role for a
human being, as perceived by this Oral Torah tradition,
is to serve as a "copartner with God in the work of
creation." No social, clerical, ethnic, religious, professional or dynastic exclusivity is imposed as a prerequisite.
The Torah is open to all and directed to all: Jews and
non-Jews, scholars and plain people, rich and poor. You
and I are given the privileged responsibility of evolving
through biblical communication to creative copartner-
ship with the Eternal in the sacred work of self renewal
and social redemption...or to use the older classic phrase,
to build the kingdom of God on earth.

Which brings us to a difficult problem. Are all interpretations of Bible equally valid? What criteria, if any, are there, what guidelines, what parameters? Or are we caught up helplessly in a labyrinth of meanings, a cacophony of voices — learned and unlearned, evolved and uncultivated —all claiming inspired enlightenment? These are not theoretical questions; they vibrate to our immediate sense of reality. Turn on your radio or television and you're likely to encounter a slick new breed of media-smart, "religious" hucksters pushing their melange of scriptural interpretations on you. Throughout America, exotic spiritual cults have proliferated in huge merchandising campaigns that feature a bewildering array of gurus, illuminati and demigods; among them even children, untouched by the modest inhibitions that restrain lesser mortals, proclaim their enlightenment to derive from direct, divine communication.

When you consider the problem more fully, you find that there are really two questions being raised here. One: who is qualified to interpret scripture? And two: what makes an interpretation valid or invalid?

The difficulty posed by the first question is more apparent than real. Of course, everyone is eligible to receive the divine inspiration emanating from the Infinite Creator to all His creatures. But are we all prepared or qualified to receive that communication and expound on it?

A brief analogy from science will clarify the point. For millions of years important messages have been beamed to the earth's surface in a continuous stream of cosmic waves from stars and galaxies racing at incredible speeds over many trillions of miles to our planet. Until quite recently, nobody on earth had progressed enough in the knowledge of physics, mathematics, astronomy, engineering and other cognate sciences to receive those messages and interpret their meaning. Even today, though everyone is theoretically eligible to deal with this cosmic communication, only those who have achieved competence in the required disciplines of learning can do the job. To confuse equality of opportunity with a doctrinaire egalitarianism is a distortion of the democratic idea. It contributes to a dangerous trend in our day, the traduction of democracy to a social instrument of promoting equal mediocrity for all. Renewing the true democratic hope for all people to fulfill their highest potential is our major social priority.

Among the earliest architects and promoters of that democratic hope were the ancient sages of Israel. They had opened the doors of their educational system universally to children and adults by the end of the biblical period in the second Jewish state. Their passion was to nourish the whole society with the living waters of Scripture. In a graceful midrash on the poetic line in Deuteronomy: "Let My teaching descend as the dew," they explained: "Even as the same dew falls upon all the diverse species of trees, sustaining each according to its individual syndrome —the vine, the olive and the fig — so the same Torah gives nourishment to every person, each according to his individual capacity."

They also set standards of excellence, intellectual, ethical and spiritual, for teachers of Torah and their disciples. They knew, what many moderns prefer to forget, that all teachers — and each of us is a teacher in our homes, offices, farms, factories, governments, laboratories, no less than our schools — instruct much more effectively by our existential being, our real values and true lifestyle, than by the lessons we teach and the ideals we profess.

Here are some of the qualities that one ought to cultivate in a Torah lifestyle, according to Rabbi Meir's famous saying: "To become a good friend, a lover of God and humankind, one who brings joy to God and people alike; to grow in humility, reverence, spiritual-

80

ity, justice, compassion, integrity and dependability; to keep far from transgression and near to virtue; to serve society with wise counsel, careful judgment and effective leadership; to develop patience and be forgiving even of personal insult; to search out the mysteries of Torah and become a mighty stream, an unfailing fountain of life sustaining waters, thus fulfilling the highest nobility granted to creatures on earth."

A formidable list! But they are not drawn up as exclusive prerequisites so much as ideal guidelines. Any reader of Talmud or Midrash knows of scholars who fall short of these qualities but whose interpretations of Bible are worth remembering. In answer then to the question of who is eligible to interpret scripture, tradition would answer: potentially everyone – in reality, those whose intellectual, spiritual and moral growth have provided them with competence and wisdom.

Our second question is far more complex and subtle. How do we authenticate biblical interpretations and evaluate them? Are there any objective criteria or is it all a matter of subjective judgment?

This problem gets us down to the bottom line of the whole biblical enterprise. If the literature is indeed sacred and holds the key to an ongoing communication between our Creator and all of us — a communication of redemptive hope for personal and social fulfillment — what then can be more urgent for us than to clarify that communication and use it? In a final word to his people, the master teacher Moses tells them: "Put your heart into all the teachings which I bear witness among you this day, that you shall bequeath them to your descendants to cherish and live by the words of this Torah. For it is not a trivial message to you; it is your very life! And by this teaching you may lengthen your days upon the land."

Seen from this perspective, we can sense more thoroughly why such massive investment of genius in western religious creativity have been poured into biblical exegesis, commentary and exposition over the past 2,500 years. It is no exaggeration to assert that the overwhelming literary output of Hebrew scholarship and Kabbalah mysticism during that entire period has been focused on this pursuit of Torah learning and interpretation.

I have been studying the literature of Torah for many years and as the old Ethics of the Fathers suggested: "Turn it over and over again for it's all encompassing; delve deeply into it, grow old and grey with it and don't ever abandon it, for you can find no better guidance." It's an encyclopedic literary output, expansive and intensive, rational and esoteric, pedantic and poetic, ethical and technical, legal and medical, historical and legendary, spiritual and sensual, and also vibrant, challenging, incisive, ennobling and sublime. Nothing human or cosmic is foreign to its concern.

As I reflect on it, the whole monumental product, for all its incalculable wealth and diversity, it reveals itself to be an organic unity. *Torah literature constitutes the authentic record of an extraordinary dialogue between Israel and God for almost 4,000 years.*

In that recorded dialogue, ideas were accepted and rejected, which should surprise no one. Every living organism accepts and rejects according to its intrinsic structure. Jews in the Bible made their debut on the world scene by vigorously advocating certain ideas about God and humans and also by opposing just as energetically the prevailing ideas about both. With enduring power, for example, they affirmed the unity of God, His spirituality, His ethical concern for justice, love and peace and His passion for human freedom. No less vigorous was their rejection of idolatry, polytheism, the amorality of

82

the pagan cults and the identification of the gods with human enslavement and social injustice.

Over many years, as the historic dialogue was carried forward from the Written to the Oral Torah, the process of authenticating ideas and expositive techniques became formalized and schematic. Methods for interpretating the sacred words of Torah developed gradually. Foremost among them were the famous Thirteen Hermeneutical Rules of Rabbi Ishmael, which became so popular as to achieve a permanent place in the daily Hebrew liturgy. The logical tools for validating biblical interpretations were refined by the tradition in its organic development from the covenant at Sinai.

Many centuries after the interpretive rules of this unique biblical dialogue between Israel and God had been accepted and creatively applied, a new vision was promulgated by the mystics of Kabbalah. There was nothing new about any of its constituent elements, but, like all great visions, the whole was intensely greater than the sum of its parts.

I refer to the profound and seminal vision of the Pardes, The Four Dimensions of Paradise, which is the major concern of this book.

In the history of ideas, it is not unusual for seers to be unaware of the magnitude of their own vision. Even when a vision becomes popular, sometimes because of its popularity, its significance can remain hidden. Such is notably the case with the Pardes. Its very name was recycled from a famous mystical agada in the Talmud a thousand years later by the major work of Kabbalah, the Zohar — Book of Splendor, which then popularized it in a completely new context. And it has been widely known ever since, as an acronym for the four dimensions of biblical exposition.

I am convinced that the wider implications of the

Pardes have eluded us to this day. The central task, therefore, which I have chosen for this book is to re-examine more thoroughly the theoretical foundation and practical use of the four dimensional Pardes in order to help us discover:

Greater personal enrichment through:

1. A more comprehensive approach to the under standing of Scripture.
2. A more authentic way to enter into the eternal biblical dialogue between God and humankind.
3. A more balanced philosophy of life and harmonious vision of human existence and fulfillment.
4. A more practical application of the Four dimensions of Paradise to bring about a more harmonious integration of the physical, intellectual, emotional and spiritual aspects of life.

Or, to use a mystical phrase that encompasses all four above: to find a more blessed path of entrance into The Four Dimensions of Paradise.

Rabbi Simeon said: "Alas for the person who regards the Bible as a book of mere tales and mundane matters. For if that were so, even we might compose one with better stories . . .But in reality, all the words of Scripture are sublime truths and soaring mysteries. Observe this. The outer garment of a person is visible to all. When fools see someone in an elegant robe, they do not look beyond it. Yet, how much more valuable than the robe is the body wearing it and, even more precious than the body, the soul that gives it life. In the same way, the Torah has a body made up of its precepts, which are called 'gufe Torah' (bodies or main principles of the Torah); that body is clothed with everyday stories. Only those of limited understanding concentrate on the outer raiment, the biblical stories, and give no thought to what is underneath. People of greater perception will regard

84

not merely the clothing but also the body within. But the truly wise, however, those who stood at Mount Sinai, they will penetrate directly to the soul, which is the real foundation of the whole Torah. And one day, they are destined to behold the Torah's innermost soul."

This forceful statement of Zohar captures the mystic's passion for searching below the surface text of the Bible, its stories and precepts, in order to draw closer to the soul and source of divine communication. It is an appropriate introduction to the multidimensional world of Pardes.

What is Pardes? The Hebrew word derives from the Greek paradeisos (paradise in English), meaning originally a park, a pleasure ground. Ancient gnostic literatures in the East and West are saturated with visions of a future paradise. For Christianity and Islam, as well as the religious traditions of India, the paradisian locus is other worldly. Classical Jewish mysticism absorbed this international term, paradise, but reshaped its ideological content to fit into its biblical prophetic tradition of messianic eschatology.

Central to that prophetic tradition is a trust in the redemptability of this world. We are not talking about a mere article of faith but an intense, active commitment, personal and communal, to the realization of a paradise on earth. To be sure, this millennial vision is not limited to our planet. Its extensions into meta space, time and being are subjects of much mystical speculation throughout the Talmud, Midrash and Kabbalah. And yet, all share in a traditional consensus — that the Bible calls us to a higher evolvement of human life on earth, from which the door is opened to eternal paradise.

Here is one of the most famous esoteric passages in the Talmud. "Four sages entered the Pardes (paradise). They were Ben Azzai, Ben Zoma, Aher (Elisha ben Abuya) and Rabbi Akiba...The first one looked and died...the second gazed and lost his mind...the third cut down the saplings (became a heretic and corrupted the youth). Only Rabbi Akiba emerged in peace."

The story contains many veiled allusions and a very substantial literature of mystical exposition has mushroomed around it over the centuries. For our discussion here, I will single out two elements.

First, we note the process by which these four scholars in the early second century, among them the leading sages and saints of their generation, enter into paradise and return to earth during their mortal lifetime. Apparently the ancient Jewish mystics had no problem with the idea that human beings could manage that ecstatic round trip. Of course, the journey was dangerous and much spiritual evolution in Torah was required but the opportunity was open to all. What impresses us is the unquestioned notion of heavenly paradise, as an extension of our earth, connected by an esoteric conduit through which two way traffic can move.

The second element of our focus is on the name of Pardes itself. I think you will be fascinated to learn how one word can hold the key to understanding a complex history of ideas.

Pardes occurs three times in the later books of the Hebrew Bible during the period of Greek influence in the Holy Land; its meaning is an orchard. G.C. Scholem quotes a Qumran Dead Sea Scroll fragment of the pseudepigraphic Book of Enoch in Aramaic to point out that the oldest Jewish esoteric books used Pardes to mean paradise. There is no question that this latter meaning of paradise became standard in classic Jewish mysticism and was so accepted in early Christian literature also.

More than 1,200 years after Qumran, Zohar took this by now venerable Pardes Paradise terminology in traditional mysticism and breathed new life into it. Its perception was ingenious. Pardes could be treated not only as a word but also as an acronym, whose four consonants PRDS are the first letters of four Hebrew words (vowels are totally dispensable in the Hebrew language; only consonants matter).

Those four words are the names of the four dimensions of biblical understanding: P is for Pshat, the literal or objective dimension of meaning; R for Remez, the allegorical, aesthetic or poetic realm; D for Derasha (same root as Midrash), the homiletic or ethical mode of interpretation; S for Sod, the mystical way of illumination.

Now the evolution of Pardes reaches a new plateau. We are taught in the Zoharic literature that the exploration of Scripture in all four dimensions leads to direct communion with the Shekhinah, the immanent presence of God. In fact, the Shekhinah is boldly called Pardes ha-Torah, Paradise of the Torah. We can sense the force of this original conception by appreciating the vital mystery of the Shekhinah in Kabbalistic doctrine; it is the tenth and final sefirah in a series of divine emanations, where all the powerful elements of the living Godhead are centered for reaching out to humanity and natural creation.

The limitations of this study do not permit a systematic investigation of the huge Kabbalistic literature on the Shekhinah in particular or the sefirot in general. Interest in this field has burgeoned rapidly and the literature is readily available to the reader. Here we make the point that the old perception of scripture, as a continuous stream of human divine communication, was elevated by the masters of Kabbalah to a new stage of meaning and purpose. Their vision of Pardes mapped out the full dimensional possibilities of that communication; it remains to this day the most complete and balanced approach to biblical understanding.

And more. It reveals the goal of the whole sacred enterprise from time immemorial: to inspire human beings, individually and socially, and guide them toward an evolving realization of their divinely endowed latencies. The Pardes is both process and fulfillment. By opening lines of communication with the biblical word, one is already on the way to paradise on earth. The more we travel this way of the four dimensions, the closer we approach the Shekhinah of God, the innermost Soul of Torah, the Paradise of eternal life.

Coming down for a while from the rarified atmosphere of theosophy, we need to examine critically one of our central claims in this book concerning the Pardes: that its four dimensions of Pshat, Remez, Derasha and Sod chart the most comprehensive course to a full and balanced penetration of the biblical world. For reasons that will become apparent in our discussion, we in the twentieth century are better equipped than all our predecessors to render fair judgment on this claim.

Apprehend God in all things,
for God is in all things.

Every single creature is full of God
and is a book about God.

Every creature is a word of God.

If I spent enough time with the tiniest creature
even a caterpillar -
I would never have to prepare a sermon. So full of God
is every creature.

Meister Eckhart

3. The Four Dimensions of Paradise Defined

FIRST DIMENSION PSHAT

בּ

The first dimension of Pshat, meaning "simple", invites us to search for the plain, literal sense of the word. What does the Bible really say? The trouble is that it's not always so simple to find the simple meaning or meanings of Scripture.

Here are some illustrations of interest. The use of Jehovah in Bible translations as divine nomenclature comes from an inadequate grasp of Hebrew syntax and usage in the first dimension of Pshat. The four Hebrew letters YHVH, which spell out the Divine Name (Tetragrammaton), are so vocalized that they may indeed be read as Yehovah. The simple truth is, however, that those vowels were borrowed from the word Adonay, meaning My Master, and assigned purposefully to the four consonants of the Tetragrammaton in order to insure against casual pronunciation of the ineffable Sacred Name. Jehovah or Yehovah is thus not a name but a substitute for the divine name.

Translations in general pose dangerous risks in the area of Pshat, not the least of which are the radical changes in popular idiom that occur in every living language. A prime example that must be rated among the very best biblical humor is the King James rendition of a line from the exquisite love poetry in Song of Songs. The Hebrew poem reads: "Sustain me with raisin cakes, refresh me with apples for I am lovesick." King James translates: "Stay me with flagons, comfort me with apples for I am sick of love." Even if the 17th Century English phrase "sick of love" meant lovesick, that doesn't help the modern reader avoid a total misreading of the literal sense, the Pshat of the biblical verse.

What makes the search for a simple, objective meaning of Scripture so complicated? For one thing, you need to equip yourself with many skills. Scholars until modern times were limited to an internal study of the Hebrew Bible because there were no comparative literatures available. Nevertheless, even for internal literary research, the knowledge of Hebrew philology, grammar and syntax, of cognate Semitic languages, such as Aramaic and Arabic, and of ancient religion, history, mythology, law, philosophy and literature were valuable tools for explaining the area of Pshat.

Today it's an entirely different story. Modern archeology has revolutionized the entire field of biblical study in ways that boggle the mind. During the past century, intensive excavation throughout the Middle East and the Holy Land have recovered previously unknown literatures of many cultures contemporary with and antecedent to our Bible. Tens of thousands of tablets, whole cities and their architectural remains, their art and artifacts have been unearthed. A staggering influx of new data from ancient Sumer, Akkad, Babylon, Egypt, Assyria, Mesopotamia, Syria, Canaan, Persia, Greece and many others have been dug up. They call to mind a suggestive line in Psalms: "Truth shall sprout forth out of the earth."

Their significance in shedding new light upon the objective sense of Scripture is already enormous and archeology is still a very young science.

America's dean of biblical archeology, the late William F. Albright, wrote a masterful summary of the archaeological contribution toward changing our views on the question of objective history in the earliest biblical books. He wrote: "Until recently it was the fashion among biblical historians to treat the patriarchal sagas of Genesis as though they were artificial creations of Israelite scribes of the Divided Monarchy or tales told by imaginative rhapsodists around Israelite campfires during the centuries following their occupation of the country. Archaeological discoveries since 1925 have changed all this. Aside from a few diehards among older scholars, there is scarcely a biblical historian who has not been impressed by the rapid accumulation of data supporting the substantial historicity of patriarchal traditions."

That was written in 1949. The past 40 years of accelerated archaeological productivity in Asia Minor have brought to light a mass of new information sustaining biblical historiography. Most notable are the epic discoveries of the past decade at Ebla, south of Aleppo in Syria, where more than 15,000 tablets were recovered from the archives of a Semitic kingdom that flourished some 43 centuries ago. So persuasive is the initial evidence from these protoHebraic records that biblical historians are leaning toward an even earlier date for the patriarchal age than previously considered.

The brilliant and meteoric rise of modern archeology to unprecedented prominence for illuminating the way of Pshat, the first dimension of Scriptural meaning, should not blind us to the reality that it is only one out of a whole new arsenal of disciplines that help the modern biblical student in this area. Anthropology, biology, chemistry, sociology, psychology, economics, geography, political science, astronomy, history, semantics, architecture, en-

91

gineering, art, metallurgy, military science, literary criticism and others, all contribute to a better, objective understanding of the Bible.

What has escaped so many of us, who are overwhelmed by this modern revolution in biblical research, is its *monumental imbalance!* Precisely here, the vision of Pardes in its broad, four dimensional perspective, can offer us invaluable wisdom. From its vantage point, we are able to see how totally absorbed contemporary biblical scholarship has become in one dimension alone — that of Pshat, the first dimension.

But the Bible is no Dead Sea scroll, no antiquarian relic unearthed from the burial mound of some lost culture. It confronts us as a Torah of Life (torat hayim) a 4,000 year tradition of vital communication for all people and all time. To be sure, the fullest application of scientific, critical analysis from every relevant discipline is indispensable for understanding it. Indispensable but not sufficient! Other dimensions of insight are also necessary.

SECOND DIMENSION — REMEZ

We have to deal with the Bible also, as immortal literature, an anthology of superb poetry, parable and allegory. After all, only a schlemiel reads poetry with the eyes of a literalist. Poetry like all art has its own dimension of truth, its own perception of reality. In essence, we are distinguishing here between two approaches toward experiencing reality: the descriptive objective and the esthetic. The former is concerned with what is demonstrably true or false; the latter with what is emotionally beautiful and stimulating or not. The techniques that are valid for one may be irrelevant for the other.

One biblical poet extols the sun that delays its orbit at high noon to prolong the day for Joshua's victory. An other poet of Psalms lauds the same sun, "as the bride-groom coming out of his chamber,

> *Exults like a hero to run his course.*
> *He sets out from one end of heaven*
> *And round he passes to the other —*
> *Nothing escapes his heat."*

Were an astronomer to protest: "Those are impossible claims. I can prove they are false. The sun cannot be delayed at noon and it does not revolve in a course around the earth." Any poet worth his salt would respond: "Your literalist, true false categories reflect only the limitations of your own myopia. Life offers wider options of experience and richer levels of meaning. Tell me, my friend, does the poem communicate esthetically to you or not? Does it speak to your heart, your sense of beauty or awaken some responsive insight of allegorical truth?"

This second dimension of Pardes, that of Remez, poetic allegory and parable, moves us into new horizons of inspired communication. Tradition records the most dramatic and enduring achievement of poetic allegory in biblical literature. The Song of Songs, esteemed by many experts as among the most splendid love poetry ever written, might never have made it into the Bible and might have been lost to us permanently, had it not been for Rabbi Akiba's famous allegory. This leading scholar in Israel during the early decades of the second century interpreted the entire book, as a sublime allegory of the eternal love between God and Israel. "Never was the world more worthy than on the day the Song of Songs was given to Israel," he taught, "for all the latter writings of Scripture are sacred but the Song of Songs is Holy of Holies."

Rabbi Akiba's effective use of Remez had solid precedent behind it. Some 850 years before, a prophetic genius, Hosea, developed the idea that the noblest model for the relations between God and Israel is the model of love. In moving poetic cadences, he interprets Israel's history, as a love story over the ages. God is the Lover who rescues His bride, Israel, from Egyptian oppression and elopes with her into the romantic desert. There at Sinai He betrothes His bride in an eternal covenant of love. Israel became unfaithful but God will forgive her and will renew His covenant of love. Hosea's metaphor became a recurrent theme among the Latter Prophets and in subsequent Hebrew literature. Akiba gave it renewed impetus when he applied it to an entire book. Later Christian allegorists popularized this same interpretation of the Song of Songs but substituted the church for Israel, as the beloved bride.

To put you in touch with a wealth of biblical communication is the the thrust of Pardes. A word, a phrase, a concept, an entire book can engage your mind on the level of Pshat and evoke in you a creative response of unexpected meanings, commitments, insights and hopes. Moving into the dimension of Remez, that same word, phrase, concept or book can delight your heart with many new surprises of expanded enrichment.

Take, for example, a graceful line from the Song of Songs: "How fair you are my love, how sweet in love's delight." Your first reaction might be: what's this doing in the Bible? As you pursue its objective meaning and context (Pshat), you will begin to confront a spiritual cultural outlook that celebrates openly the sacred joy of love. So far from the uptight, guilt-ridden denigration of physical love as carnal sin in many religious traditions, the Bible views both the physical and spiritual as part of the same integral unity of divine creation. Physical love no less than spiritual love is to be sanctified in joy. Enlarging upon Rabbi Akiba's allegory in the second dimension of Remez, the saintly founder of modern

Hasidism, Rabbi Israel Baal Shem Tov commented some two and a half centuries ago upon that verse from the Song of Songs and said: "A man cannot know in depth the love of God until he has experienced the love of a woman."

How can we discuss biblical allegory without referring to the famous story of Balaam's ass? Imagine the miracle of a talking donkey and one that speaks fluent Hebrew at that! What self-respecting agnostic can resist the temptation to sneer at this scripture? You remember the story. Encamped along the eastern bank of the Jordan River, the Israelites were poised to cross over into the Promised Land at Jericho. Balak, king of Moab (today's Kingdom of Jordan) sends to Syria for the well known prophet Balaam and offers him a handsome fee to curse these children of Israel. Balaam undertakes the job and mounts his donkey for the trip to Moab. A divine messenger, visible to the animal but not to Balaam, blocks the road with his sword drawn. The donkey refuses to budge (as burros are wont to do). Balaam whips the animal and here's the classic dialogue.

"And the Lord opened the donkey's mouth and she said to Balaam:

~ What have I done to you that you beat me three times?

And Balaam replied to the donkey:

~ Because you disobeyed me.

Then the donkey said:

~ Am I not your trusted ass whom you have ridden all these years? Have I ever done such a thing to you?

And he answered:

~ No.

Then the Lord opened Balaam's eyes and he saw the messenger standing in the way with sword drawn."

Over many centuries, the agonizing polemics between fundamentalist defenders of this miracle and their scoffing adversaries have all been a protracted exercise in futility. From the perspective of the Four Dimensions, we can see that both sides dealt with this exquisite piece of allegory in a prosaic and unimaginative literalism.

We have here a perfect example of Remez, the second dimension of Pardes. Maimonides and Saadia Gaon, both leading rationalists in medieval Jewish philosophy, interpret this entire passage as dream symbolism. I see it as a literary masterpiece of satire! The Bible is poking fun at Balaam, the greatest heathen prophet of his day and Rashi, with his sure instincts for a biblical phrase, grasps this meaning in his commentary. "Such a famous seer... his ass sees more than he!"

And what makes Balaam so worthy of scorn? His readiness to sell his prophetic gifts for a fee. Something important is being said here that marks a new stage in ancient religion. All prophets of antiquity were professionals; their theurgic powers to invoke blessings or maledictions were for sale and many of them were on the royal payroll. Hebrew prophecy emerges out of that stage to honor independent spirits, teachers of religion and ethics who are beholden to no earthly powers but stay free to serve the truth of their inspired visions.

Typical of this new breed of prophets is Amos who lived more than 2,700 years ago. He was not afraid to speak out against the King of Israel, prophesying that "Jereboam will die by the sword and Israel will be exiled from its land." Reacting angrily to this treason, Amaziah, the priest of Beth El, tells Amos to go back to Judea where he came from. Maybe there he can make a living as a prophet but not in Israel. Amos sets Amaziah straight: "I am not a professional prophet, nor the son of a prophet but a cattleman and a caretaker of sycamore trees. And the Lord took me from behind the flock and said to me - "Go prophesy to my people Israel."

That man was worthy of inaugurating the Golden Age of Hebrew prophecy, one of those rare, intense periods for the flowering of spiritual genius. Its achievement is recorded in the books of the Latter Prophets, which spanned two and a half centuries in ancient Israel to become a major and permanent legacy for the whole human race.

And so, it turns out that the strange episode of Balaam's ass, under the lens of Remez, yields a profound insight of allegoric truth. I might add that it has proven also to be a gold mine for humorists. One of our best contemporary wits allowed as to how much our world has changed. In former times, it was considered a miracle that an ass could talk. Today in our world of mass media, we no longer find it miraculous or even unusual when asses speak!

You may appreciate my own postscript to this Balaam affair. It strikes me as an allegory within an allegory, a kind of multileveled REMEZ. Balaam comes to curse but remains to bless. With consummate artistry we are taught that God cannot be manipulated, not by the most talented sorcerer and magician. Balaam and Moses are the two major symbols of contrast in prophecy. One uses all the magical paraphernalia of ancient religion, including "snake enchantment" to cash in on his divine powers. The other receives this highest scriptural tribute...he is not called liberator, nation-builder, lawgiver, statesman, military leader, master teacher or religious genius, all of which were true. Moses is honored as a "faithful servant of God" and that says it all!

You ought to know in this regard that the fifth book of Moses marks the first effort we have on record to separate magic or sorcery from religion. "Let there not be found among you any who make their son or daughter

pass through fire, no diviners, soothsayers, snake en-
chanters or magicians, no spellweavers and no mediums
to consult ghosts, familiar spirits or the dead. Anyone
given to these practices is an abomination to the Lord. Be
wholehearted with the Eternal, your God." Not bad advice for us today when so many people are falling into
every crazy neoprimitive cult. We need to learn all over
again that pure religion, refined from the dross of magic,
involves faithful service to God — not using Him but
being used by Him.

*The greatest revolution in our generation is the discovery
that human beings, by changing the inner attitudes of
their minds, can change the outer aspects of their lives.*
William James

THE THIRD DIMENSION — DERASHA

ד

Before we enter this dimension of ethical and homiletic wisdom, I want you to know that you are not bound
by any sequence of priorities on your voyage. Above
all, don't wait until you have examined all interpretations on record within one dimension before moving on
to another. The literature of divine colloquy in each of
these four dimensions is so very rich, you can hardly
explore it all in one lifetime.

Derasha (like midrash) derives from a Hebrew root
meaning to search, to seek out, to investigate. It is the
oldest among the four modes of biblical interpretation
and originally included them all. Here are some illustrations of this classic, interpretive process in the third
dimension.

"Justice, justice shall you pursue in order that you
may live..." asserts a scripture in Deuteronomy. Why is
justice repeated twice? To teach you that justice should
be followed both in word and deed, whether to your
profit or loss, to your kin and to the stranger. Not even a
just purpose is served by injustice; both means and end
must be just. An especially worthy goal to seek today in
all systems of justice both individually and collectively.

This last derasha exposes in one bold flash of insight
the moral bankruptcy of Marxist-Leninist ideology and
all totalitarian doctrine sanctioning every crime against
humanity – even terror, torture and mass murder – as a
legitimate means for achieving political power. How
we've been deceived into swallowing the unjust dictatorship of the proletariat, as a transitional means to that
presumably just goal of a classless, socialist society. Today, after millions of people have been liquidated in
Communist states and tens of millions dehumanized all
over our planet, we are left with an obscene perversion

of means and end. Stripped of all its sloganized masks, the real face of this golem communist paradise reveals itself to be nothing more than a ruthless dictatorship over the proletariat. 1991 will be noted as a memorable year, when the yearning for freedom and individuality became explosive throughout the world.

Note also the latter phrase in this scripture: "Justice, justice shall you pursue *in order that you may live."* It is saying (according to an ethical interpretation in the third dimension) that human life cannot survive without justice. An ancient sage in the Ethics of the Fathers explained: "The sword of violence and death ravages society when justice is violated or perverted.

You and I can resonate to that. We have seen the sudden decline of our legal system and the equally rapid upsurge in violent crime all over America and abroad. Invest in crime — suggested a Wall Street pundit recently — it's the major growth industry in the world today!

Let me present a second type of Derasha, as we find in the famous biblical law, "an eye for an eye, a tooth for a tooth. . ." You may ask: is this primitive law of retaliation compatible with scriptural ethics? How can it be considered divinely inspired?

What you may not know is that this law was not applied literally but was interpreted in the third dimension to mean: the value of an eye for an eye, the value of a tooth for a tooth. If, for whatever reason, someone injured another's eye, tooth or any bodily part, the court was to determine the appropriate damages to be paid by the offender. Parenthetically, those monetary damages were to include, not merely the assessed value of the injury, but also the cost of therapy, loss of earnings, personal pain and indignity suffered.

How can a biblical law, which seems so clearly to require physical retaliation in kind, be interpreted to

100

mean financial payment in value? The answer can clarify for you the whole world of Derasha, the Third Dimension of Pardes.

It's not enough to read the Bible literally (first dimension) or allegorically (second dimension). If you are entering into a reciprocal communication with God, you are challenged to search out the fullest intent of His divine word. Especially is that true of law, which touches the heart of interhuman, ethical relationships. I will give you a digest of the extensive literature on the legal interpretation of this scriptural law. Not to worry — you don't have to be a professional student of the law to enjoy its logic and creative, ethical power.

Several passages in scripture deal with the problem of injury to animals and to human beings; those verses shed light upon one another. In Leviticus, human injury is discussed along with injury to animals and, since the Bible expressly provides for compensation in the case of animals, the same must be intended for human beings. Homicide is the only exception to that rule because for that crime scripture ordains specifically: "You shall take no compensation." But for all other human injury, we may infer logically that compensation is acceptable.

What is more, that interpretation is supported by Hebrew semantics. The original Hebrew text of the Bible reads: "ayin tahat ayin — an eye in place of an eye". How could the removal of an offender's eye take the place of his victim's eye? Obviously Scripture is not talking about punishment by mutilation but by *just compensation*. And if you're still in doubt, another biblical verse makes it clear that "tahat" refers to monetary payment: "He shall surely pay for an ox (tahat) in place of an ox."

Need I add that physical mutilation of a defendant's eye, tooth, hand or foot would violate every major principle of biblical ethics? Way back in the prehistoric age of

THE FOUR DIMENSIONS OF PARADISE

Noah, scriptural law had already prohibited animal mutilation; how much more so for human beings! I might
add that archeology has dramatic proof for the humane
progress of ancient near eastern law on this question
even before the Bible! Some fragments of what may be
the oldest legal code in the world, the laws of Ur–Nammu,
King of Sumer, were translated and published about 25
years ago. They date back more than 4,000 years, long
before Mosaic laws, and contain a list of compensatory
damages for human injuries: ten silver shekels for a foot,
two thirds of a silver mina for a nose. . . not a very
impressive valuation of human limbs. Reading this and
corresponding lists of payment for the loss of limbs in
today's insurance contracts will convince you that things
haven't changed too much in four millennia. At any rate,
the old argument that justice in early biblical times was
much too primitive to allow for anything but a literal
application of "an eye for an eye," is utterly demolished
by this one archaeological find alone.

But, you may ask finally, who needs all this mish-
mash of archaeological legal casuistry? If scripture meant
the value of an eye for an eye, why didn't it simply say
so? The answer is to the point. If biblical law mentioned
only the monetary value of a limb, as Ur–Nammu's
Sumerian code did, the rich might become quite insensitive and even casual about injuring people. After all,
they can well afford to pay for the damages. In so phras-
ing the law, "an eye for an eye," scripture wants to
proscribe such insensitivity, to teach that the eye of the
poor is equal in value to the eye of the rich. It's telling us
to be very careful about inflicting physical harm upon
any human being even as we ourselves would not want
to be victimized by others.

Why have I led you through this brief tour of
scriptural law and lore? For one thing, to give you an
authentic taste of the very rich possibilities of divine

communication in this Third Dimension of Derasha. The whole scriptural word of God needs to be studied and interpreted — both its laws (midrash halakhah) and its narrative portions (midrash agada).

To guide you in your interpretive research, millennial tradition developed rules of logic and exegesis. Hillel's Seven Rules, the Thirteen Principles of Rabbi Ishmael (by far the most authoritative formulation) and Rabbi Eliezer Ben Joseph's Thirty-Two Postulates are among the best known. These are worthy of further exploration.

Ultimately this entire system of communicating with God through the interpretive study of His biblical word, rests on a foundation of ethics. A line in Psalms proclaims that "the word of God is purifying," which is explained in a classic derasha to mean that "All the teachings of scripture were given to purify the human race." As metal is purified by removing its dross and refining it to higher states of purity, so the biblical communication of God removes all the crude vestiges of sub humanity from us and helps us evolve into higher states of ethical nobility.

In this Third Dimension of Paradise, all 613 commandments of Scripture, the whole biblical literature itself, every sacred word and letter becomes a divine communication of ethics...not moral theory but the real life practice of ethics that moves us forward in our personal and social evolution.

Is there any journey more indispensable for you and me and our society at large than this one into the third dimension? What future can there be for an ethical lifestyle of Neanderthals in the nuclear age?

Include friend and foe in your petitions, for how can one ask God for blessings which he does not want others to have?
Orhot Tzuddikim, 15c Ch.9

ב

"The words of the Torah are formed like the nut. Just as a nut has an outer shell and an inner kernel, so every word of Scripture contains external truth and inner mystical truth."

This brief statement from a commentary on the Book of Ruth gives you a straight forward passage on your journey into the fourth, the mystical dimension of biblical communication with God. What do we mean by mystical? I will tell you first what it is not. Don't confuse mysticism with theurgic magic, divination, enchantment or witchcraft. All are expressly forbidden by Scripture, as "an abomination to the Lord."

Nowhere is authentic mysticism more clearly reflected than in these simple cadences from the Psalms:

"As a hart yearns for the waterstream,
So my soul longs for You, Lord.
For the Eternal, the Living God,
My soul thirsts exceedingly.
When will I come near
To behold the face of God?"

At the core of every religious tradition stand the mystics. They are not content with a casual relationship to God, the kind that suffices for most believers. Some occasional experiences of divine light, a few peak moments of soul nourishment cannot satisfy their hunger for closeness to God. The transcendent gods of philosophy leave them cold. Theirs is a consuming passion to attach themselves in a direct and continuous relationship to the Eternal Infinite God of all reality and truth. Not even communication with a distant deity would be enough.

Which calls to mind a story that became a classic. During his visit to the White House, then Prime Minister Begin of Israel noticed three colored phones on President

Carter's desk: one red, one white and one blue. He asked:

~ What are these phones for?

~ The red phone is a direct line to the Kremlin, Carter explained. The blue one is to you in Jerusalem and the white phone connects directly to God.

~ How interesting! May I use that white phone?

~ Help yourself. But I must tell you it's terribly expensive...one million dollars for three minutes.

~ Much too high for us, said Begin, we're a small country with a big budgetary deficit. Maybe next time, thank you.

About a year later, Carter came to Jerusalem and saw the same three colored phones on Begin's desk. Now he asked:

~ Where do your three phones connect to?

~ The blue one to your office in the Oval Room of the White House; the red one to Cairo and the white one directly to God.

~ Is your white phone as expensive as mine?

~ No, here it's quite inexpensive, Begin replied. In Washington, D.C., a call to God is long distance. But in Jerusalem, it's only a local call!

The mystic has a problem in dealing with the biblical word. All words are basic linguistic symbols which we humans assign to the things we perceive through our five physical senses. And everybody knows how very limited our sensory perception really is. Even allowing for the broad extension of our five senses by modern technology, the question remains: how reliable are scriptural words, as limited symbols of human language, for communicating God's infinite wisdom? Do they confine us to a mere surface understanding of the Bible within our fixed boundaries of sensate experience? What about the vast regions of truth and reality that lie beyond our cognitive perception?

For the mystic, therefore, the problem of interpreting

scripture is not just what the words mean, but *what are they covering up?* What is the inner wisdom, the kernel of God's infinite truth, for which the biblical words and letters are but an outer shell, a communication of finite, imprecise symbols?

Here's a fascinating example of how one letter by itself can yield whole worlds of hidden insight in this fourth dimension of mysticism. Why, the Zohar asks, does the Bible open its epic story of creation with the Hebrew letter, bet, which is also the number two? To teach us that cosmic creation took place on two levels: one above and one below.

What is more, there is a divine connection between these two cosmic realms: the supernal world beyond the limits of our senses and the world of visible reality we live in. Our world seems hopelessly fragmented; to us, everything exists in differentiation and disunity. We are separated from society, nature and God... even from our own inner selves. And yet, if you reflect more profoundly, you will realize that all this fragmentation is external. Below the surface, all things are one in God. His unity is the substance that underlies and interconnects all creation. You may note, in that regard, the Hebrew name for God chosen for the opening verse of Genesis begins with the letter aleph, meaning one.

The mystics of Kabbalah extend this idea to affirm a strikingly dynamic relationship between God and all of us, His human creatures. Using a very subtle form of Gematria (a study of the numerical value of letters to uncover the hidden meaning of words), they point out that the Hebrew letters in Adam's name and in the sacred name of God (the Tetragrammaton) both equal 45. This equation reveals much more than the biblical conviction that everyone of us shares in the divine essence. Just as both sides of an equation may act reciprocally upon each other, so the inner world of a human being can and does interact with the esoteric world of the Eternal God.

A very bold claim is made here for the cosmic role of every human being. It presents you and me with a challenge of unique power.

Historically the main drama among mystical traditions has centered largely around the individual saint in personal search of an ecstatic union with God. That striving for devekut, the individual soul reaching out to embrace God in a continuous flow of love and bliss, is no less prominent in Kabbalah. But the intense, social conscience of biblical prophecy demanded more. In that biblical tradition the spiritual journey is not just for some few saints but for the whole community; all are mandated to become "a nation of priests and a sacred people."

What is more, you cannot traduce the mystical dimension of personal growth to an escapist love affair with God. This world of ours cries out for healing (tikun olam). Everywhere there is suffering, hatred, misery, hunger, disease, violence, oppression and destruction. All our accumulated wisdom in the natural and human sciences (first dimension), in the arts (second dimension) and in socio-ethical philosophies (third dimension) have not diminished our fragmentation and despair. We feel overwhelmed and impotent.

Centuries ago, the Kabbalists saw this crisis as one of the spirit no less than the mind. They defined our challenge in a symbolic equation of reciprocal interaction between humanity and God, a symbolism that speaks vigorously to our condition today.

It's telling you and me that we need to discover the immense power within us, the great leverage we command for good or evil, for unity or divisiveness...or to use a Kabbalistic phrase, for "healing the broken vessels" of our world.

107

Each one of us on earth shares in the essence and power of God. In His unity, we are all created to be one—at one with ourselves, with all other human beings, with nature and with God. All are linked together as in a chain; if one link is severed, the whole chain loses its integrity.

A mystic commentary on the well known scripture, "You shall love your neighbor as yourself," makes the point that your neighbor is a vital part of yourself; both of you are interconnected within the universal essence of God. When you hate anybody, rob, exploit, shame, attack or murder—whom do you hurt? Yourself and the whole organic system to which you belong. Conversely, when you help someone, encourage and befriend, extend kindness, compassion,hospitality and forgiveness to any person—whom do you benefit? Yourself and the world.

In this fourth dimension the Bible serves to open up important lines of communication between you and God. It unites you with Him and the unity of His cosmic purpose.

You and I have the power, the capacity to transform ourselves and our society but we have lost the vision. And without a unifying vision, we withdraw into isolation, fear and a paralysis of will. Who doesn't feel these days the loneliness, apathy, powerlessness and futility of life? It's an awesome world we observe through our telescopes, unbelievably vast and explosive, rushing everywhere and going nowhere. The aching, the longing for some warmth, some purpose, some light—we all feel it, not just the mystics.

Concerning that light, which scripture tells us God created on the first day, the Zohar raises an interesting question. What light are we talking about? Wasn't the sun created on the fourth day in the Genesis story?

The answer is suggestive and compelling. When God first said: "Let there be light," He was referring to the infinite, divine light of the Bible, that mystical light, which pulsates, creates and renews the whole universe.

The resplendent light of biblical wisdom in all four dimensions, which connects you in direct, reciprocal communication with God, can restore for you and all of us the vision we have lost. It can unite us with Him in a unity of cosmic meaning. Not just mystics and saints, but everyone of us is capable of drawing close to Him and receiving His inspiration. In this Kabbalistic symbolism, we are being told that you and I are worthy of entering the Four Dimensions of Paradise, that we can achieve fulfillment for ourselves and serve to advance the redemptive healing of our society.

The first stage of this journey, the introductory tour, ends here. Now we start an extensive exploration into the Four Dimensions of Paradise to uncover some treasures of biblical wisdom that have evolved out of divine human communication over millennia. I invite you to examine those great treasures which have been assembled from remote places among biblical and post biblical literatures in all four dimensions.

We will enter a world of wisdom and enlightenment that has been almost exclusively the domain of mystics and scholars: the world of inspired communication between God and humankind by means of the scriptural word. This journey touches the central purpose of our book, to open God's communications system to all His children, as originally intended. In Book III, you are welcome to share in this enrichment and prepare yourself for creative experiences in scriptural communication with the Eternal.

Enough preparations. It's time to start our trip through the Four Dimensions of Paradise.

> *What lies behind us and what lies before us are tiny matters compared to what lies within us.*
> Ralph Waldo Emerson

> *Every house a temple, every heart an altar, every human being a priest.*
> M. Lazarus, Ethics of Judaism

BOOK THREE

*Creative Explorations
in Four Dimensions*

In Tribute to
Rabbenu Rabbi Samuel Penner

Creator:

You constantly create worlds, life and beings

You create us and we are glad to be.

You give us love and You seek our love.

You give us vast powers in Your creation.

Give us the wisdom to use it well.

We need Your guidance to wield it

in harmony with Your will

and in harmony with all Your creatures.

Help to set right   what we have spoiled

        to heal   what we have injured

      to console   what we have saddened.

Rabbi Zalman M. Schachter – Shalomi

and

Eve Rochelle Penner Ilsen

1. Creation

GENESIS 1:1-4
In the beginning of God's creation of heaven and earth, the world being formless and void, with darkness over the deep and a powerfull wind sweeping the waters, God said: "Let there be light." And there was light. And the Lord saw that the light was good...

DIMENSION OF OBJECTIVE MEANING —PSHAT

Before we get into some exciting issues raised by these famous verses, let's focus for a moment on a grammatical item of interest. You probably noticed that our translation above differs somewhat from the old versions that read: "In the beginning God created the heavens and the earth." Rashi, a classic biblical commentator of medieval France who was famous for his advocacy of Pshat, the plain literal meaning of scripture, pointed out that the opening words of Genesis are in the construct state. Therefore, the translation above.

Of course, he is not just making a technical point of syntax. He goes on to draw the logical inference that Scripture does not box us into a rigid time sequence for the creation of the world: first the heavens, then the earth and the light and so on. Otherwise how can you explain the heavens created on the second day if they were already created on the first? Even in antiquity, it was noted that Scripture does not maintain a fixed chronological order. Some events, chapters and even books, which appear later in our editions of the Bible, are in fact dated earlier chronologically. It's refreshing to know that, although many people are uptight about the Bible, the biblical style itself is not uptight but hangs loose in its chronology, that "it speaks in the style of human language." As for Rashi's grammatical comment, many other scholars agree with him and I think he is right.

Which brings us to the big question everybody asks when they open the Bible. How does this account of creation jibe with the cosmological theories of modern science? Many people who have been exposed to contemporary ideas in astronomy, astrophysics, geology and biology, decide right here that the Bible is outdated and irrelevant; whereupon they often close the book never getting past its first chapter.

When I was a boy growing up in the Bronx, I had a friend whose father was a pickle wholesaler and that's just the way he did business. He would taste the first pickle off the top of the barrel. If it suited his taste, he bought the whole barrel; if not, he walked away from it. I don't know whether this is the best way to operate a pickle business (my friend's father actually went bankrupt and got into another business) but I do know that it's a naive and self-impoverishing way to approach the Bible. It's naive because you don't have to be an expert in social sciences or literature to know that you cannot impose simplistically your own contemporary modes of thought upon an ancient literature; you must first understand the inner world out of which that literature evolved. It's also self impoverishing because you cut yourself off by such hasty prejudgment from the one literature whose enduring power for life enrichment is without analog in all of recorded history.

114

That is perhaps the chief value of those Four Dimensions of paradise. They open you to the inner world of the Bible and reveal its infinite possibilities for your self-evolvement in a balanced wisdom of intelligence, art, ethics and spirituality.

Much of classical wisdom is intuitive, whereas scientific knowledge is empirical. Still I can't help wondering about the uncanny scriptural intuition that describes the start of cosmic creation with a burst of light into a formless, dark void. By some inexplicable coincidence, that age old intuition forms a basic premise of the universally accepted Big Bang Theory of creation in modern astronomy. According to this theory, a primordial atom, a gigantic fireball was exploded about 15 or 20 billion years ago, when our world was born. The stuff released from that cataclysmic blast, we are told, still rushes outward in all directions at unimaginable speed, generating new stars and planets as well as their complex biochemical processes for nurturing life. Ours is a universe that pulsates with endless creativity, as the ancient talmudic masters perceived: "Continuously every day, God renews in His beneficence the work of cosmic creation."

I must add that new evidence has been accumulating lately to challenge the current Big Bang Theory. Several astrophysicists of repute now feel that it needs to be revised. Such is the flow of authentic science and it should tell us something about glib, oversimplified answers to questions about science and scripture. If you're looking for the latest scientific theories, don't go to the Bible! Consult the journals of scientific research and evaluation. Neither scripture nor religion was ever intended to encompass this vast scientific enterprise or to limit its horizons for new discovery.

Upon closer examination, it turns out that our original question of how the Bible jibes with modern scientific theory may not even be pertinent. Were Scripture to do no more than espouse today's most popular scientific theory, it must surely become irrelevant tomorrow when that theory is replaced by new evidence.

What then do we come to the Bible for? For much more than empirical knowledge. We are so overwhelmed with the awesome breakthrough of scientific method in this one dimension that we tend to ignore our modern lack of progress in the other dimensions of life: the esthetic, the ethical and the spiritual. This gross imbalance now threatens the survival of all life on our planet and lies at the root of so much joylessness, suffering, anomie and despair in our society.

This is what you come to the Bible for, as the four Dimensions of Paradise help you perceive it. Here is a literature that summons you and people everywhere to grow in all the dimensions of your divinely endowed potentialities.

I am convinced that the problem for biblical literature is not now and never has been a problem with science. That misconception must surely go down as one of the supreme blunders of all time. The scriptural problem we need to deal with is a semantic one. Like all other literatures, the Bible makes use of available data, concepts and stories within the cultural world of its time. How else could it speak except "in human language?" Our essential problem is how to translate that language of biblical times in order to communicate its inspired ideas and values *for all times*.

All right. Let's get into that. What are the opening lines of Genesis really telling us in the first, objective dimension of Pshat? Nothing less than the most revolutionary idea to come out of the ancient world!

The monotheistic revolution, which Genesis 1 proclaimed in antiquity, may seem rather tame to us today.

Big deal, you may be thinking, so one God created the world. So what? Your so what is a useful question; it sharpens our focus upon those lasting achievements of the Genesis revolution that changed the whole world outlook of humankind.

More than 700 gods are listed in the Babylonian pantheon records at Shuruppak (now called Tell Farah) which archeologists estimate to have been compiled about 4,700 years ago – and the list is probably not complete. Now that's a lot of gods to serve! The Babylonian faithful must have had a formidable problem trying to satisfy the legion of gods in their world some 4,000 years ago.

But the concept of one Creator God involves much more than a mere triumph of mathematical simplification. The classic Babylonian epic of creation, Enuma Elish, which is much older than our scriptural Genesis, records the violent and cruel battles of the gods preceding creation. This cosmogonic myth reaches its climax when Marduk seizes the goddess Tiamat in a huge net and crushes her skull with his merciless club. He cuts her monstrous carcass in two and fixes one half on high to become the firmament of the heavens and the other half, the foundations of the earth below.

Less violent but no less crude is the old Egyptian myth of creation that describes how Atum, the chief god of Heliopolis came into existence out of the primordial fresh water ocean, Nun, before heaven and earth were created. Being alone, he masturbated in order to create a companion, whereupon he conceived and vomited forth the god Shu (air) and the goddess Tefnet. From their union issued Geb and Nut (earth and heaven) the parents of Osiris and Isis, Seth and Nephthys.

All this was rejected and transcended by the monotheistic thought of Genesis. Why? To begin with, we need to understand that these theogonic myths of antiquity were never a matter of abstract theological speculation. They were dramatic stories reflecting the real attitudes of peoples, how they saw life and the world around them. Those imaginative mythologies about the gods and their violent strife form a vivid statement on how the ancients perceived the powerful and often cruel forces of nature and society. In that perception, war, xenophobia, violence, oppression and cruelty were validated by divine example, having been built into the system of reality from the beginning.

It should not surprise us, therefore, to find a mood of predetermined fatalism in the polytheistic world view. Even the gods were not free but subject to primordial powers which had generated them. That is why magic was everywhere tied into pagan religion because serving the gods was not enough; you had to learn the techniques for controlling or allying yourself with those primal forces to which even the gods themselves paid obeisance. As magic is characteristic of polytheistic religion so was despair its prevailing tone all over the ancient Middle East.

With a simple majesty Genesis addresses itself to both. It proclaims the uniqueness as well as the unity of God, the supreme universal Creator. Dissenting from all known mythologies of the Tigris-Euphrates, Nile and Hellenistic cultures, the biblical God stands alone. He has no ancestry, no family connections, no divine consort, son-god or daughter-goddess. No magic can prevail over His will; in fact, all magic is an abomination to Him. What scriptural monotheism tried to accomplish was to remove magic and fatalistic despair from religion and replace it with a resurgence of hope for the redemptive possibilities of human life.

The most revolutionary achievement of Genesis, however, was to universalize religion and its concept of

God. The ancient gods were local deities – associated with some region, power or phenomenon in nature, or with some individual, family, tribe or nation in society. The monotheistic revolution, which Genesis set in motion and all biblical literature reinforced, had a universal vision – so avant-garde that it has not yet been realized thousands of years later – the harmonious unity of God, nature and society.

And yet it did succeed in gradually transforming polytheistic societies and paving the way for a new cultural synthesis based upon this premise: that our world is indeed a universe. It would require a whole series of books to tell the story of how this radical idea of one world, one Creator and one human family has influenced our mode of thinking in all branches of learning and literature to this day. But one brief observation here is essential, as we conclude this first section of Pshat.

If the polytheistic profusion of gods had divided people and confused them, the monotheistic claim of Genesis could now unite humanity with a new hope and purpose. The old system had given mythic validation to war and xenophobia. The new theory could now start a millennial effort to bring all people together and advance the cause of peace.

DIMENSION OF ALLEGORY - REMEZ

Creation adds up to much more than the objective sum of all its quantitative parts in time and space. Essential to every creative act is the qualitative spirit of art. As we enter the second dimension of Pardes, we explore some new insights into the same opening verses from Genesis, now perceived through the symbolism of art, poetry and parable.

On this level, creation is approached as a cosmic work

119

of art by the Supreme Artist. Sensitively the ancient sages of Midrash reinterpret a biblical line, "There is no rock like our God"; by a slight revocalization of the word tsur- rock, to tsayar - artist, the passage is rendered: "There is no artist like our God." All creative inspiration flows from Him, which is why scripture frequently refers to artists and artisans as being filled with God's spirit.

The first century Alexandrian philosopher and famous biblical allegorist, Philo Judaeus, stresses the esthetic significance of Genesis. "No one, whether poet or historian, could ever give adequate expression to the beauty of biblical ideas respecting the creation of the world, for they surpass all the power of language." Why is light so primary that it was created on the first day? "Because light is surpassingly beautiful. And what is his explanation for the prevalence of order in the divine plan? Because, "there is no such thing as beauty in disorder"– an opinion that many modern artists would hotly contest.

Which calls to mind a great story about a young man who came looking for a wife to the shadchan (the marriage broker, a widely used professional in the old days). He said,

~ She does not have to be a rare beauty, but at least attractive and presentable.

~ I have just the young lady for you. She's pretty as a picture.

The date was arranged and kept. Early the next morning, the young man stormed into the shadchan's presence, his face ablaze with fury.

~ Pretty as a picture, you say? A harelip, corkscrew nose, cleft lip, one eye higher than the other, balding, with strands of weedy hair protruding from her ears and sunken chin, to say nothing of the rest of her revolting body. Some picture!

120

~ Young man, smiled the shadchan. What's the matter with you? You don't like Picasso?

Another allegorical gem uncovered by the Midrash centers around the opening word of Scripture, "B'raysheet," which can be translated, "with the beginning." Now a verse in Proverbs informs us: "With wisdom God founded the world." According to the well-known expository rule that one related biblical verse can shed light upon the interpretation of another, the sages propose this symbolic meaning ~or Genesis 1:1: " With wisdom did God create heaven and earth."

The idea is popular throughout biblical literature. The poet of Psalms rhapsodizes: "How manifold are your works, O Lord, all of them You created with wisdom." Greek philosophy in its mainstream also holds that wisdom, intellect and reason touch the essence of God and the process of cosmic creation. Einstein expressed that same concept when he wrote of his "rapturous amazement at the harmony of natural law, which reveals an intelligence of such superiority that, compared to it, all the systematic thinking and acting of human beings is an utterly insignificant reflection."

But the midrashic masters were talking about much more than cerebral wisdom. They meant also the "wisdom of the heart," which includes emotional, esthetic, moral and spiritual wisdom. All of these, they suggest, together with intellectual wisdom, were instrumental components in the divine creation of our world.

How does this allegory strike you? For me, the Psalmist says it best: "I find joy in Your word as one who chances upon great treasure. Here is a classic example of creative communication with God via the biblical word, illumined and magnified in this second dimension.

After all, the first lines of Genesis are amazingly

121

sparse on details about cosmic creation. Only the leanest skeleton outline is given to describe what has to be the greatest event of all time. You can raise a thousand questions about what is written and what is omitted. And above all those questions is this one: how does it all relate to you and me? The ancients saw in such questions an open invitation to enter the biblical process of creative communication with God. Their allegoric interpretation of Genesis 1 to identify an all embracing wisdom, as the instrument of universal creation, speaks symbolically to us.

How? An old talmudic observation with surprising contemporaneity tells us that "every human being is a miniature universe." If we humans really are little worlds of untapped potentialities — as cellular biology and all the human sciences will confirm — then the issue for each of us is this: what kind of a job are we doing to develop that personal world entrusted to us? And collectively what are we doing with the whole galaxy of human microcosms we call society?

To these questions, Genesis offers a vital response. If wisdom was the divine instrument for creating and renewing the universe, it is no less indispensable for us, human co-creators on earth, in the advancement of our personal and social worlds. Nothing on earth is more destructive than the abandonment of intelligence, of disciplined reason and balanced wisdom. That truth is written large across the decades of our century consumed by so many irrational, anti-life compulsions of fear, hatred, violence, cruelty, war and genocide. The key to survival is wisdom; it also points the way to fulfillment and joy.

Probing here in the second dimension, we find many more precious allegories on the same verse and we'll pause to examine a few of them. "Why was the letter, bet (second letter of the Hebrew alphabet) chosen to be the opening letter of Genesis? A preposterous question, you may think, unless you recognize the premise that every word, every letter of Torah is divine communication to be mined for treasures of wisdom in all dimensions. The letter Bet is also the number two and it alludes to the two worlds that were created in the beginning: our finite world and the infinite world of eternity.

Another symbolic reason for the use of bet to start the biblical text in Genesis 1:1 is to teach us that the dual, male-female syndrome was woven by the Creator into the very fabric of our world by original design. This perception is shared by ancient Chinese thinkers who expressed it in a wide application of the Yin-Yang principle.

Inveterate optimists, the teachers of Midrash noted that bet is also the first letter of the word Bracha - blessing. They hear the Holy One Blessed Be He saying: "I will create my world with the bet of blessing and maybe then it will endure." What, you say, "maybe then it will endure?" Can't the Omnipotent God assure our world's survival? The inference is clearly no. You remember the grand biblical challenge: "Life and death I set before you, the blessing and the curse; choose life that you may live, you and your descendants." God's investment in His human creatures may be gaged by the freedom of choice He grants them; it's an investment of considerable risk.

He minimized that risk by using the bet of blessing to begin the creation of our world. You might think logically that the first letter would have been more appropriate but that letter, aleph, starts the word, Arirah, which means malediction. It had to be bypassed the sages explained, in order to dispel any theological or philosophic misconception about predestined evil in this world. But the ultimate option of life or death, blessing or misery, He left to us.

In a classic Jewish folk tale, Chayim turns to his friend Joseph with a deep sigh and says:

~ It's an utterly mad, irrational world, Joseph, I thought I had it all figured out logically. I bought two businesses, a grocery store and a dry goods store... figuring either-or. Either people live, in which case they must patronize my grocery store, or they die, in which case my dry goods store will be busy providing burial shrouds. How come, with both businesses, I can't make a living?

Joseph pondered the question at length and finally his eyes lit up with an answer.

~The reason is simple, my friend. Nowadays, people neither live nor die. They struggle to survive!

If we humans choose to inflict misery and destruction upon ourselves, Genesis is telling us in this allegoric perception, the responsibility for that choice is ours. God offers another option; it's built into His creation and always available — the bet of blessing.

What kind of an idiot, you ask, would choose misery over well-being? Don't ask! History is drenched with the blood shed by a pitiless human irrationality. I can't imagine a time in all of recorded human experience when people inflicted more agony upon people than our century. This midrash doesn't tell us why. It simply says there is a better way... and that way of blessing was woven into the biblical message of creation.

DIMENSION OF ETHICS AND HOMILETICS — DERASHA

It may very well be true that no single influence upon human ethical development has ever been more powerful than the first sentence in Genesis. Why? Because it affirms that our lives have purpose, that we are not here on earth by some chance confluence of meaningless events.

"A person sees a beautiful pillar," the midrash points out," and responds: blessed be the quarry from which it was hewn. Regard also our splendid world and say: blessed be the Creator who shaped and refined it." Rabbi Akiba told his students: "Even as a house testifies to its builder, a garment to its weaver and a door to its carpenter, so does the universe testify to the Holy One Blessed Be He Who created it.

Think of Genesis 1:1 as a revolutionary pronunciamento for the claim that life has meaning and value. It vigorously negates a popular view, captured in Shakespeare's immortal line, that life is "a tale told by an idiot, full of sound and fury signifiyng nothing." "A man who regards his own life and that of his fellow creatures as meaningless, wrote Einstein, "is not merely unhappy but hardly fit for life."

What will motivate such a person to grow as an ethical human being? In this third dimension, Genesis 1:1 takes on a new significance as the foundation on which the whole moral system of biblical communication stands. After all, why bother to invest yourself — your time, energy and substance — in being just and kind to others, whose lives are meaningless and worth nothing? No doubt some few souls of exceptional nobility can cultivate the moral strength to transcend their nihilism. Bertrand Russell, one of our century's most persuasive nihilists, urged us Prometheus like to defy the gods that don't exist and strive for moral intellectual excellence despite the utter hopelessness of our fate. His exhortations sound hollow today.

Most people who shed what they regard as their naive illusions about life's meaning or value, do not become better human beings for it; they tend to become narcissistic self-idolaters. Taking care of Number

One in lifestyles that range from egocentricity to ego-mania is thus fast emerging as the great passion of our time.

Self-idolatry comes across at first as comedy but its aftermath is disaster. What is funnier than a self-inflated fool so totally wrapped up in himself that he cannot see what a small package he is in the real world? An ancient legend has it that when King David had completed his poetry of psalms, he boasted: "who has ever sung more beautiful songs of praise to God than I?" At that moment, a frog leaped into the royal chamber and said: "David, don't think you're so great. I croak out my songs of praise to God with each breath I take every moment of my life!" A wise Hasidic master taught: "there can be no room for God in people who are all stuffed up with themselves."

But self-idolatry has run amok in the twentieth century at a cost in death, suffering and devastation exceeding that of all precedent history. A parade of self-deified buffoons and mass murderers, Hitler, Stalin, Mussolini, Mao, Idi Amin, and more— the list is dreary and contemptible — all once commanded absolute power to devalue human life and reduce the sacred individual to a servile golem.

They are gone but their genocidal legacy remains with us to haunt our memory and alert us to the idolatrous menace of unlimited sovereignty.

Genesis 1 proclaims that God alone is sovereign and that all life created by Him shares in His sanctity and illimitable value. Its clear ethical inference is that all human power whether granted to individuals, political parties or national governments, must always be limited by higher ethical mandates of justice and compassion.

We will have learned nothing from the unspeakable

126

anguish of our century if we do not learn this: the price of playing god is too high.

How many families are destroyed and personal lives crushed by self-worshipping, petty tyrants? They are a plague to every institution and a curse to themselves. On the international scene they heap on us all the harrowing maledictions of Deuteronomy. One cure, parenthetically, is not on that list because it was then unthinkable: the liquidation of all life on earth. The unthinkable is now in our hands.

A rich lode of many other ethical ideas from the same opening phrase in Genesis can be explored in this third dimension. We will assay a few of them. Every builder, a popular midrash points out, needs blueprints for his construction. Which blueprint did the Creator use for His universe? The Bible. We are also told in a legend that God had created many worlds previously but they did not endure. Ours persevered because He designed it according to His biblical plan. And so, the sages conclude, if humankind matures to live by the just and compassionate teachings of Scripture, we can build a paradise on earth. If not, we will turn our planet back to its precreational chaos of dust and ashes.

How many intuitions recorded 1,800 years ago speak so meaningfully to us today? Those sages blended intuition with logic. In this, their moral commentary upon Genesis, they were drawing an analogy between the laws of nature and the laws of society. All things in nature — from the massive galaxies to the tiniest sub-atomic particles — are governed by the precise physical laws of their Creator. Any violation would destroy the whole system. Just so, they reasoned, is human society governed by precise ethical laws set forth in the divine communication of Scripture. If we continue to violate them, we consign all human society to the final, apocalyptic blast.

127

I admire the sensitivity of people who concern themselves with the survival of every rare species — animal, bird, fish and plant life. But we must also care about saving millions of men, women and children throughout the world from being savagely starved into extinction. We are only a generation removed from the systematic murder of six million Jews (among them 1,200,000 children) in Nazi gas chambers and crematoria all over Europe. With few saintly exceptions, the world community was inconceivably silent.

More than 3,000 years ago, we were taught these ethical laws in scripture: "You shall not stand idly by at the shedding of your brother's blood." "Let your brother live together with you." "Justice, justice shall you pursue that you may survive." "You shall not hate your brother in your heart... you shall love your fellow human being as yourself." Those moral laws and others were built into the creation of our world no less than the laws of physical motion and mass. In violating them, we not only threaten our survival; we prove ourselves unworthy of surviving at all.

The whole human family will have to face up to this ultimate, moral challenge and the ancient sages spell it out graphically: "Every individual should say — the world was created for me!" What they were saying was that everyone of us counts in shaping the future of our planet and its life systems. How we think and act are not trivial matters of personal whim. They affect our lives directly.

We know how vitally every person counts in maintaining our physical ecology. One savage can devastate our natural resources and life systems. The same holds true of our social ecology. One ethical primitive can wreck a family, a community, a society. On the other hand, one mature and concerned person can act effectively to renew nature and society. *Everyone* counts and nobody can remain neutral in this issue of survival.

A sailor who survived the bombing of Pearl Harbor wrote to his mother in Brooklyn describing all the horror and destruction around him. His mother wired him back immediately: "My son, make sure you stay out of it!" No one will be able to stay out of a third world war or escape its thermonuclear fury. Your personal maturation into ethical responsibility begins when you decide: "This world was created for me and I have a personal role to play in shaping its future."

One more exquisite little homily before we move on to the fourth dimension. It opens with the question: why did the Holy One Blessed Be He start His Torah with the letter bet of Genesis and finish it with the letter lamed in Deuteronomy? The answer is that these two letters spell out two words that define the two basic ethical ingredients of a civilized human being. The first word is lev, meaning a heart. It tells us that the whole Bible from beginning to end is committed to helping us cultivate a heart of love and compassion for all.

"What is the most precious achievement of a human being on earth?" asks Rabbi Yohanan ben Zakai in the Ethics of The Fathers. Among the many answers given by his students, the master chose this one by Rabbi Elazar: "a good heart," warm and empathetic to everyone. All other virtues are contained in it. That's what the ethical dimension of Paradise is all about, to ennoble us with the generosity and loving kindness of a good heart.

But that's easier said than done. There is a second word formed by those two letters, bet and lamed, the word bal, which means - no. Here is the other side of the coin that tells us something many of us don't want to hear these days. I refer to the unpopular truth that without self-restraint, without the inner strength to say no to yourself when necessary, it's no use prattling about a generous heart or ethical growth or even human survival.

What really separates mature adults from children?

129

Certainly not their age. You and I know many old people, who never emerged out of a lifelong, arrested adolescence — and we may even recognize ourselves among them. What all have in common, these kids of whatever age, is a weakness of character. You'll find them eating, drinking, smoking or drugging themselves to death. You name the temptation; they can't resist it! The life of unbridled self-indulgence, a modern revival of the same self-idolatry that has been historically the last stage of every civilization's decline, is becoming the major trend of western culture.

Is there anything more counter current to modern lifestyles than the idea of delimiting your freedom by personal commitment? To say yes or no to yourself for any higher sanction than your most immediate gratification? Yet that is precisely the thrust of an important biblical message in this third dimension: to say yes to kindness and no to cruelty, yes to generosity and no to pettiness, yes to compassion and no to vengeance, yes to justice and no to oppression, yes to honesty and no to deception, yes to encouragement and no to despair, yes to friendship and no to hostility, yes to love and no to hatred, yes to life and no to destruction.

"Monotheism means not only the positive search for unity, but also, negatively, the refusal to set man in the throne of God."
Roth

Indulged, self-deified children regard their unlimited personal freedom, as the measure of all things — an illusion that must end disastrously. How long, for example, can a world community survive, which accepts violent terror and the wanton murder of innocent human beings, as legitimate tools of political action? On the other hand, to abandon your freedom and dissolve your sacred individuality in total, uncritical subservience to any cause is the way of sub-human slaves.

A mature human being searches for the lifestyle of balance between personal freedom and social responsibility. That path is never easy but the ethical wisdom of divine inspiration is also never distant.

Before we move into the next dimension, you may want to pause and reflect upon your explorations thus far. How do you feel about these issues which we have only begun to examine? The real purpose of this book, as you probably realize by now, is to encourage you to do your own exploring, thinking and evaluation. And always be ready for surprises. Thus, what appeared at first to be a charming homiletic play with two hebrew letters turns out to illumine a major area of moral wisdom in the third dimension. And that too is one of the unexpected delights of your voyage through the Four Dimensions of Paradise.

> *Moral Action is the meeting place between the human and the divine.* Roth

What does an ethical style of life most strongly affirm?

For mystics, the opening line of Genesis is tantalizingly brief. I mean, economy is commendable but seven Hebrew words to encompass the whole creation of heaven and earth? And even if you add the 30 verses that complete this first biblical chapter, what do you have more than a tiny, mouth-watering hors d'oeuvre to whet your appetite for the full banquet? We should not be surprised to find an immense literature of mystical commentary exploring beneath the letters, words and lines of every sentence in Genesis 1. During this, our first journey into the fourth dimension, we must limit ourselves to some selected treasures of spiritual wisdom and intuitive genius culled from Midrash, Talmud and the Kabbalistic books.

God, the Creator Who confronts us in the first sentence of scripture, what is His essence? That's a crucial question for the mystic whose probing to understand and draw closer to God is the soul-passion of his life. The poetry of Psalms captured that passion in a movingly simple line: "My soul yearns for God more than night watchmen yearn for the dawn." He knows that his finite intelligence can approach the ineffable mystery of God only through a limited symbolism of spiritual communication but that doesn't discourage any mystic from pursuing his restless search.

And there is something of that mystic in all of us. At the age of five, an exceptionally gifted boy, who later was to become one of the greatest Hasidic masters, was told by a visiting sage:

~ My son, I will give you a gold coin if you can tell me where God is.

The boy replied:

~ Rabbi, I will give you two coins if you can tell me where He is not!

132

You might think that of all people, the scientist is least likely to get involved in the mystical quest but you'd be wrong. Einstein says it best: "The most beautiful experience we can have is the mysterious. It is the fundamental emotion which stands at the cradle of true art and true science. Whoever does not know it and can no longer wonder, no longer marvel, is as good as dead...A knowledge of the existence of something we cannot penetrate, our perceptions of the profoundest reason and the most radiant beauty, which only in their most primitive forms are accessible to our minds— it is this knowledge and this emotion that constitutes true religiosity."

That sense of wonder at the unfathomable grandeur of our world is not limited to mystics or scientists. You and I have experienced it. Who among us has not been curious about the ultimate reality, the creative power that brought our universe into being and sustains all its organic life and inorganic matter under the most precise laws? Many rich treasures of insight were amassed by probing the biblical creation epic in this fourth dimension; they all derive from that same curiosity.

Over and over again, we find the essence of God perceived throughout mystical literature in the symbolism of light. "Scripture teaches that the Shekhinah (Immanent Presence of God) is all light and that out of the Shekhinah's radiance was the light created on the first day to illuminate the world forever."

Another midrash suggests that the heavens were created by divine rays of light. "From what source were the heavens formed? From the light of God's raiment they were shaped and spread out like a curtain. And they continued to expand until He said to them: "Dai-enough!" That is why God is also called by the name Shaddai – the One who said: Dai! And where do we learn of this origin of the heavens out of the supernal light of God's raiment?

133

From the scriptural passage of Psalms:

> *"Praise God, O my soul.*
> *Eternal, my God, You are very great,*
> *Clothed with glory and majesty*
> *You cover yourself with light as raiment*
> *And stretch out the heavens like a curtain."*

You can't overlook the remarkable affinity between this ancient intuition about God settling finite boundaries to the expanding heavens and a current theory of astrophysics, which views our universe as expanding to its maximal limit and then contracting back to its original point of creation every 20 billion light years or so, in cycles of explosion and implosion. But if you're tempted to jump to any premature conclusions about this relatedness, I would advise you to resist that temptation. In reading any mystical text, we must always be on guard against a literal approach that misses the point of its suggestive symbolism.

The symbol of light, however, as the essence of God and the instrument of His unending process of creation and inspiration is relevant not only to modern thought; it's a major theme of Kabbalistic expression and many other mystical systems. One of the earliest books in Kabbalah is known as Sefer Bahir, the Book of Radiant Light and the classic bible of Kabbalah is entitled the Zohar - Resplendent Light.

And what makes light so popular a symbol among mystics of every tradition? Of all matter and energy in the universe, light is the most revealed and the most hidden, the most obvious and the most elusive, the most real and the most esoteric, the most pure and the most beneficent, the most casual and the most indispensable. Its first place, therefore, in the biblical sequence of creation is altogether appropriate.

But the Kabbalists, searching more deeply into the

134

opening words of Genesis, achieved a major new perspective concerning the inner light of divine reality.
There is no more basic and original concept in all of
Kabbalah than the divine mystery of the Ten Sefirot – a
bold revelation of God's inner being and creative process
unfolding through ten emanations of His light.

What are these ten stages of divine emanations?
Even as I list them I ask you to keep in mind that they
represent profound esoteric symbols of what in philosophy or rational theology might be analogous to the
attributes of God. To treat them literally is simplistic and
meaningless. Here they are:

1. Keter - The supreme crown of the En Sof, the
   Infinite One.
2. Chochmah - The wisdom of God.
3. Binah - Divine understanding.
4. Chesed - The love and kindness of God.
5. Gevurah or Din - The power and justice of God.
6. Rachamim or Tiferet – The compassion and
   Beauty of God.
7. Netsach - The eternity of God.
8. Hod - The majesty of God.
9. Yesod - The foundation and creative energy
   of God.
10. Malchut or Shekhinah - The kingdom and imma-
    nent presence of God.

Quite obviously, an adequate discussion of the many
symbolic meanings and imaginative applications of these
Ten Sefirot are beyond the scope of this book. You are
advised to consult the definitive studies of our time in this
area by the ranking scholar of Kabbalah, Gershom G.
Scholem. For our purpose, some few comments are offered to shed light upon how they relate to our exploration
of Genesis 1 in this mystical dimension of Pardes.

From time immemorial biblical readers have noted

that the Hebrew name for God, in the first line of Genesis, Elohim, has a plural ending. Many advocates of polytheism have tried to authenticate their beliefs here but to no avail. You see the verb, "created" - bara — is in the singular which would require that its subject, Elohim, also be in the singular, since Hebrew syntax requires that the noun and verb have the same number. What is more, the entire Hebrew Bible from Genesis to Chronicles is committed intensely, as every school child knows, to an uncompromised monotheism.

Why then is the divine name, Elohim, used here when so many Hebrew alternatives with a singular ending were available? The mystics of Kabbalah came up with a theosophical response of much depth. They perceived the One Eternal God as uniting within Himself all the divine powers which premonotheistic peoples formerly ascribed to their many gods.

Interestingly enough, the Hebrew words elim and Elohim actually mean powers as well as gods. So according to this Kabbalistic view the unique cosmic drama of creation was generated by the unity of all powers within the living God (Elohim) that are symbolized by the Ten Sefirot; all of them were energized by the pulsating emanations of His light.

Has ever a person lived who did not at one time ask: what was the world like before creation? For many mystics, the answer is that the Infinite God filled all cosmic space (pleroma) in the precreational world. Scripture supports this idea: "For the heavens and the expanses of the heavens cannot contain Thee..." Translated into the symbolism of Kabbalistic thought, we are told that all the ten sefirot of God's inner being filled the precreated universe in a dynamic unity and balanced harmony — all suffused with His supernal light.

When He determined to create our world, according

to the Kabbalists of Safed, He withdrew, contracted and concentrated His infinite being to one intense point of light. That intense concentration is called tsimtsum in Hebrew, a concept that goes back to the fascinating intuition of some mystical sages in the third century. Precisely this point of God's immense power and light is "the beginning" of creation, a process that started within the divine unity of being and extended into cosmic space.

A recent discussion was brought to my attention, in which some prominent physicists, astronomers and scientific cosmologists were speculating on this same question: what preceded the Big Bang, that primordial explosion of such concentrated power and intense brilliance as to set in motion all the creative materials that shaped our world. That discussion and even its semantic symbolism is surprisingly close to these Kabbalistic ideas on creation.

From a scientific viewpoint, such questions about precreation may not be legitimate but that doesn't diminish our curiosity or inner urge to speculate about them, even if they are beyond our ability to resolve. That sense of curiosity and an intuitive, imaginative capacity to go along with it is one of the Creator's great gifts to His human creatures. It also enriches our communication with Him in this fourth dimension.

Do you think that these Kabbalistic ideas about the inner being of the Creator and the process of His cosmic creation are nothing more than metaphysical speculation? Or imaginative flights of fantasy recorded in a rich symbolism? Probe more deeply and you will find those intuitive symbols communicating a vital wisdom for human life. I choose one of many such spiritual insights of wisdom those mystics derived from the first line of Genesis and comment upon it briefly as we close this section.

137

All human beings, according to the talmudic masters, are copartners with God in the work of creation. We are not fulfilled unless we can create. The powerful Kabbalistic symbol of tsimtsum contains an intuitive insight of immense importance to deepen our understanding of the creative process and its value in our lives.

For me, the most vital of all is the quality of love and compassion that is conceived here as an essential ingredient of creativity. In order to create our universe, God disturbed His own inner being, which had filled all cosmic space with the ten sefirot of His light, and troubled Himself to the point of withdrawal, contraction and intense concentration. So great was His divine love to share His infinite life that He created new life forms in great abundance and provided a generous ecology for their sustenance.

Here is a paradigm for human creativity, a parable for all. Take the trouble to withdraw from your own self-absorption and share your life with others by a creative act that adds to the richness of life. You fulfill thereby the divine essence of your humanity. Choose whatever area of your interest or competence, there are no limits to the intensity and variety of such creative work. Through it, you can achieve the noblest expression of love.

In this view, the whole world may be seen as the laboratory of God, and all of us human beings as among His most exciting experiments. But we are not alone. All living forms and inorganic things everywhere pulsate with His four dimensional light of truth, beauty, goodness and spirit. That is the thrust of Isaiah's vision: "Holy, holy, holy is the Lord of hosts (the galaxies of stars and all cosmic matter) the entire universe is filled with His glory." One of His names is Ha-Makom, the Place. He is everywhere, yet He has His own space.

138

A Sunday School kindergarten teacher asked her tots one day
~ Where is God?
A little boy in class startled her by answering
~He is in the bathroom.
Hesitatingly the teacher said
~ How do you know?
And back came the response
~ Because every morning daddy stands outside the bathroom and yells: "My God, are you still in there?"
Like all authentic folk humor, this story has some depth. Scripture speaks of God, "who dwells among us even in our state of uncleanliness." When we appear in our own eyes to be most distant from Him, He is close by. A Hasidic master was once asked the same question
~ Where is God?
    And he answered
~ Wherever you let Him in. That's the heart of
    Genesis and the mystery of creation.

> *He who loves, brings God and the world together.*
> Buber - At the Turning Point 1952

Who gave you your invulnerable life, your strength, your speed, your joy? Samuel Taylor Coleridge

2. On Human Creation

GENESIS 1:27
"And the Lord created man in His essence - In the essence of God He fashioned him, male and female did He create them..."

DIMENSION OF OBJECTIVE MEANING — PSHAT

ndulge your most lavish fantasies for a moment and fancy yourself possessing the combined wealth of all the oil in OPEC. Even that staggering conglomerate of riches cannot approximate your true worth as a human being!

That's the plain meaning of this biblical statement on human creation. Every member of the human family is infinitely precious. Created of God's essence, we all share in His immeasurable worth.

In an amusing way, biochemistry has finally caught up with the grandeur of that idea. For years we were led to believe that our chemical worth was about 98 cents each at the corner drug store. And that old saw had some limited validity. If you added up the retail cost of all chemical elements that go into the making of a human body — oxygen, hydrogen, carbon, nitrogen, calcium, phosphorous and others—your total amounted to 98 cents only a decade ago. Runaway inflation has since increased our value to a new high of ten dollars per person.

But now we learn how simplistic that reckoning had been all along; the numbers were right but they didn't tell the whole truth. After all, the living components of a human body consist of much more than its basic chemical elements. They include highly complex substances, such as enzymes, proteins and hormones. Only a few of them can be reproduced synthetically at prices you won't believe.

An enzyme called acetate kinase costs $8,860 a gram (1/16 of an ounce). Bradykinin, a potent dilater of bloodvessels that delicately combines variant forms of protein, sells for $12,000 a gram. For the terribly rich, there's prolactin, a hormone whose street price is $17,500,000 per gram. Most of these vital substances which our bodies produce without fuss cannot be synthesized in the laboratory as yet. A biochemist at Yale University, fantasizes that, if we could somehow manufacture all the subtle parts of one human cell and put it all together, the cost might approximate 6,000 trillion dollars ($6,000,000,000,000,000). Multiply that inconceivable figure by the many trillions of cells in your body and you grasp the precise meaning of the Bible's statement on human creation.

All this bonanza may do nothing to raise your Dun and Bradstreet rating or your credit at the bank, but the fact is that you are priceless! We are not accustomed to valuate ourselves so realistically.

If your body value alone exceeds the aggregate wealth of the planet, what is your personal worth as a whole human being — body, mind, soul and spirit? No less infinitely valuable, according to this biblical concept, than the essence of God which forms the core of our creation. Every person is a universe in miniature, declares an ancient midrash and that is confirmed by modern cellular biology. Therefore, the Talmud concludes, to save one human life is to conserve the whole world and conversely, to destroy a single person is to devastate the universe.

142

You have probably noted by now that my translation of the Hebrew text above uses the phrase, "essence of God," in preference to the more popular image of God. I am in agreement with Maimonides, who asserts in his "Guide To The Perplexed" that the Hebrew zelem does not mean an image but an essence. The words toar (form) or demut (likeness) would have been more appropriate, if scripture had intended to represent Adam's creation in the divine image. But the issue goes beyond semantics. Ideologically the phrase divine image is incompatible with the biblical sense of human creation. After all, the vigorous opposition to imaging God in any physical form, human or non-human, runs through Hebrew scripture as a major motif.

Built into the stylistic flow of Genesis 1 is the view of human creation as an event of supreme cosmic importance. Adam is the last to appear in an evolutionary progression from inanimate things to plant, marine, bird, animal and finally human life. Everything else was fashioned by divine fiat — "Let there be...and there was." Adam, however, was created after deliberate divine forethought. He is presented as the crown and glory of creation.

That, of course, never inhibited any humorist from poking fun at him. Man is the creature God created after a hard week's work clearly in a moment of divine fatigue, opined one of our contemporary wits. An ancient talmudic sage asked: "Why was Adam created last?" His answer was on target: "So that whenever people become arrogant, they can be reminded – even the lowly gnat took precedence over you in the order of creation!"

After her daughter's wedding ceremony, Golda Meir, the celebrated Prime Minister of Israel, whispered to her new son-in-law:

~ Adam was better off than you.

~ In what way, asked the bridegroom?

~ He had no mother-in-law.

Other wits have added to the list of Adam's good fortune. He never had to listen to his wife extolling the virtues of all the better men she could have married. And if he came home late, he could always answer Eve's recurrent complaint:

~ And you have the nerve to tell me you still love me?

~ Of course. Who else?

In all the ancient myths of Mesopotamia and Egypt, there is no analog for the pre-eminence bestowed upon human life in the Genesis narrative. Pagan gods fashioned human creatures capriciously or begrudgingly, as menial slaves to their divine masters. Our scripture in its most literal sense rejects that crude perception of human life altogether. It opens thereby a new era in the struggle for human dignity which spans all the centuries and embraces the hopes of every generation.

Grant me the ability to be alone,
May it be custom to go outdoors each day
among the trees and grasses, among all growing things
and there may I be alone, and enter into prayer
to talk with the one that I belong to.
Rabbi Nachman of Bratzlav

THE DIMENSION OF ALLEGORY — REMEZ

How do we understand this obscure phrase, "ZELEM ELOHIM," the essence of God? It symbolizes our individuality, according to one of my favorite talmudic passages. "This is to tell the true greatness of the Holy One Blessed Be He. For we mortals mint many coins with the same die and every coin is exactly alike. But

144

the Eternal created all humans in the mold of Adam and not one of us is identical to another."Here is a fascinating claim that we encounter God's essence not in our similarity to others but in our uniqueness. What makes you specifically you — unlike any other person who ever was, is or will be — is the divine within you.

Society presses us to conform like coins minted to exact specifications. And that process has reached an advanced stage in totalitarian states where dissent is anathema and people are being ground into robotized clones. This was surely not God's design for creating human beings. He chose to implant within each of us a divine spark of individuation.

You may have some difficulty with this idea. Who has not dreamt of a time when all human differences will vanish and one nation, one religion, one culture will prevail over all? But that is no democratic dream. It's a totalitarian nightmare couched in the very language of the old Nazi slogan: "ein Volk, ein Kultur—"(one nation, one culture)." The way of democracy is not to wipe out individual or group differences but to cherish and enjoy them!

All my life I have resonated to this ancient talmudic allegory on the creation of Adam because it projects a timeless vision: the authentic democratic goal of unity within diversity.

Without unity, diversity erodes into chaos — people doing their own thing unconcerned for the human family. Lacking diversity, unity takes on the dull prison gray of uniformity we see spreading cancerously today all over our planet. Both are pathways to despair. Our most basic challenge is to put them both into harmonious balance – the free pursuit of personal and group expression together with the responsible contribution of all to a cooperative enrichment of society.

"If I am not for myself," said the sage Hillel, "who

145

will be for me? But if I am only for myself, what good am I? And if not now, when?"

Another classic allegory on the divine essence within us holds it to be our mind, our intellect. Nobody asserts it more forcefully than Maimonides in his Guide To The Perplexed. "The intellect which emanates from God to us is the link that joins us to Him. You have it in your power to strengthen that bond, if you so choose, or to weaken it gradually till it withers."

The most sacred business of your life is the cultivation of your mind and your heart. Here Maimonides stands in the mainstream of biblical tradition. Scripture enjoins: "Know Him in all your ways," and that signifies all the areas of knowledge open to you. To do less is to diminish the essence of God in you.

We are not accustomed to associate religion with intellectual freedom much less with a commitment to universal education. It is appalling to note how comfortably the great religions of the east and west were able to live side by side with mass illiteracy and ignorance! All manner of beliefs and rituals were decreed for the faithful, as sacred duty, but not the cultivation of their minds. That is why we find it so refreshing to encounter Maimonides in the eleventh century, when medieval Europe had sunk into a Dark Age of illiteracy and superstition, codifying lifelong education as the most sacred of all religious activities.

A thousand years before Him, the sage Hillel had taught: "One who does not study, sentences himself to death." And in this epigram, you will find much truth. When you cut yourself off from intellectual stimulation and growth, your body may continue to show all the vital signs of life but it is no longer the life worthy of a human being. Petrifying your mind is to diminish God's essence within you, according to this allegory; it

146

impairs your connection with the cosmic source of all life. Therefore, look to learning, the sages taught, for the power to renew your life continuously.

IT CAN BE DONE AT ANY AGE.
A primer for ambitious people which proves that there is no preferred age for great accomplishments,

At the age of...
19 SCHUBERT composed "The Erkling"
22 MARCONI was granted first patent on wireless telegraphy
23 NEWTON discovered the laws of gravitation
31 EDISON invented the incandescent lamp
38 KEPLER discovered the laws of planetary motion
41 COLUMBUS discovered the New World
46 FRANKLIN invented the lightning rod
53 GUTENBERG finished the Mazarin Bible, the first printed book
56 COPERNICUS discovered the earth's movement around the sun
69 WAGNER composed "Parsifal"
73 THOMAS MANN published his novel, Dr. Faustus
75 EINSTEIN published his field theory
77 CLEMENCEAU presided over the Versailles Peace Conference
80 MOSES led the people out of Egypt
90 SARAH gave birth to Isaac

ADULT EDUCATION by T.F.James

DIMENSION OF ETHICS AND HOMILETICS — DERASHA

What does it mean, in this Third Dimension, to be created in the essence of God? Of all possible interpretations, scripture explicitly presents one, an ethical one, in the exquisite story of the Garden of Eden.

Eve, you may remember, savors the fruit — no apple is mentioned — from the tree of knowledge of good and evil, in response to the serpent's seductive challenge: "The Lord knows that the moment you eat of it, your eyes will be opened and *you will be like God knowing good*

147

from evil." As if to reinforce this idea, when Adam and Eve had both partaken of the forbidden fruit, we are informed: "And the Lord said: indeed, the human being has become like one of us knowing good from evil."

Clearly God's essence is identified biblically as our capacity for ethical judgment. To grasp the full power of that concept requires a deeper understanding of the story.

Is the theme of an ancient garden paradise unique to Genesis? Of course not; it abounds in the old literatures of the Near East which modern archeology has made available to us. The oldest on record is a Sumerian myth inscribed upon a tablet about 5,000 years ago that celebrates in verse a garden of immortal gods in the "land of Dilmun, a pure, clean and bright land which knows no sickness or death." This paradise was for gods only, not for mortals.

In many Semitic versions of these paradise myths we encounter the symbols of a tree of life or plant of life. They reflect a strong preoccupation among ancient societies with the wish to transcend death and attain eternal life. For them, to be like the gods meant to be immortal.

Our Garden of Eden has its tree of life too but now its role is diminished. Here the main spotlight focuses upon the tree of knowledge of good and evil. Scripture shifts its emphasis away from the prevailing mythic absorption with mortality and immortality directing its major concern to the problems of morality and immorality. Not to live forever but to live nobly was seen as the measure of God's essence in us. Hebrew scripture turned away from the perennial fixation upon death and life after death; its thrust was an ethical commitment to life on earth.

The story is told of an elderly Jew in Chicago who attended an ecumenical meeting. The auditorium was filled when he arrived and the old man sat down in

148

the front row; now he would be sure to hear the Protestant, Catholic and Jewish speakers clearly. That night the crowd was aroused by a fiery evangelist who preached on the heavenly bliss of life eternal. Orchestrating his message to an intense high, he thundered

~ All of you, my brothers and sisters, who want to go to heaven, rise up and come with me!

The entire audience stood up as one, except for this old Jew in the front row. The minister turned to him and asked

~ Brother, don't you want to go with us to heaven?

~ Of course, came the response. But between you and me, Reverend, what's the rush?

He was right. Our prior commitment is to the unfinished business of life on earth. In order to conduct that business effectively, according to Genesis, every human being has been granted what no other living species enjoys: the divine gift of moral discernment. How to cultivate that gift in our personal lives, in our relations to other people, to all life, to nature and to God is the all-consuming passion that embraces the whole biblical enterprise and enflames its every page with the thrill of being human.

You may ask: if Adam and Eve were created originally with the divine essence of moral judgment, why did they become aware of it only after tasting the forbidden fruit? And the answer is that ethical discernment can never be bestowed upon us full blown, as a prepackaged gift. It is built into our system as a latent capacity that needs to be developed and tested in real life. By trial and error, that is how we grow ethically from childhood into old age.

And nobody ever attains ethical perfection. "There is no perfect saint on earth who has done only good and has never transgressed," the wise Ecclesiastes assures us. In the Garden of Eden our ancestors failed their first test and took the consequences of that failure. But they also grew in moral awareness and assumed responsibility for their lives. Perhaps human history really begins when they leave their sheltered Eden and undertake that awesome task – inherited by every generation of their descendents – to fashion a new paradise all over the earth.

The cutting edge in this third dimensional view of our divine essence reaches into the ultimate human problem: how to confront each other, how to relate to one another. The obvious biblical answer is: as members of one global family.

The sages asked:

~ Why was one Adam created and not others?

~ For the sake of peace, they answered, so that nobody can say: my father is superior to yours.

This sense of one human family everywhere on our planet is a major ethical theme of scripture. It is also a consensus shared by contemporary human sciences.

But that is not enough! After all, some of the worst aggression, ranging from verbal and unspoken hostility to the most violent crime, occurs within the family. Recently I was present at a golden wedding anniversary when the bride was asked

~ Did you ever think of divorcing your husband during those 50 years of marriage?

~ No, she said firmly. Murder...often but divorce never!

From Cain to us, cruelty and fratricide have cursed our intrafamily relations. Has any century surpassed us in human suffering, torture, starvation and murder? Which generation of our forbears has amassed the unspeakable agony of Auschwitz, Biafra, Uganda, Cambodia, the Gulag camps and more and more?

As I write these lines, the news media report on self-defense schools for the aged cropping up all over

America to teach older men and women how to confront their most feared predators: teenagers. In his last line of prophecy, Malachi envisioned a time when the hearts of young people and their elders will be turned toward each other in reciprocal love. That age he saw as a portent of the messianic redemption. If he was right, we're in for a much longer wait than any of us had anticipated.

The unanswered cry of Malachi documents, our social failure to advance on the scale of moral evolution even to the extent of family good will: "Have we not all one father? Has not one God created us all? Why do we deal treacherously each against his brother?"

But the noblest quality of all human relations, in the biblical view, is attained when we treat each other in full awareness of the sanctity of God with which everyone of us is equally endowed. That is why scripture teaches: "You shall love your fellow human being as yourself, I am the Lord." What's that last phrase, "I am the Lord," doing there? It seems superfluous and is generally omitted whenever this golden rule is cited. Yet it is really the heart of the commandment.

I am convinced that this rule to love your fellow human being is inseparably connected to another, "You shall love the Lord, your God, with all your heart, with all your soul and with all your might." Scripture is saying that, if you really love God, you cannot hate or harm any human being. Look at the text sequence in Leviticus 19. First, "you shall not hate your brother in your heart... you shall not take vengeance nor bear a grudge." Then, "you shall love your fellow human, as yourself, I am the Lord."

To love another person is not always easy — our world is filled with unlovable scoundrels. However, to love anyone as yourself may not even be possible, ex-

151

cept for saints...and biblical ethics were intended for plain, unsaintly people like you and me. The difficulty, I believe, is one of translation. The Hebrew, Kamocha, can mean "as yourself" but also "who is like you." If you accept the latter meaning, as I do, the golden rule now reads: "You shall love your fellow human who is like you, I am the Lord" (who created you both in My essence) In this rendition, Scripture is not legislating the quality of our love. Who can generalize on any individual's capacity to extend love? The supremely important thing is to be aware that every person you face, and even those you may never face in remote areas of our planet, are all of the same divine essence as you, being worthy therefore of your compassion.

What, you may object, are we prattling about compassion and love for a Hitler, Stalin or Idi Amin? Doesn't that sort of Pollyannaism border on the obscene? I remind you that biblical and talmudic laws prohibit the use of torture even against the most sadistic criminal. They are to receive their full punishment by law but no torment or hatred. Otherwise, we would become like them, desecrators of God's essence in humankind. No matter how repulsively a man befouls the divine essence in himself, we may not join with him in that defilement.

In the ethics of Hebrew scripture, love is no substitute for justice. On the contrary, they are both so interdependent that one can be dangerous without the other. Lacking justice, love is worse than fraud; it is a pseudopiety that perpetuates injustice, delays moral growth and impedes self regeneration. On the other hand, justice untempered by compassion may be inhuman.

No life of quality is possible without love. Even the nudnick (an endlessly persistant nuisance) the coarse and the unevolved stand in need of compassion. (A more virulent prototype is the phudnick – a nudnick with a PhD).

Those mystics who studied the numerical values of Hebrew letters for a deeper understanding of the biblical word, pointed out that the letters for love (ahavah) add up to 13 and the four letters of God's name (the Tetragrammaton), total 26. What does this signify? It tells us, they explained, that wherever two human beings relate to each other in love, they are blessed together with the presence of God. And that is another hidden meaning of "I am the Lord" at the end of the golden rule. If any two human beings confront each other in an act of loving kindness, I the Lord, am there with them.

And the Kabbalists add: "In love, the secret of God's unity is found. Love unites the higher and lower realms and elevates everything to the place where all is one."

Take one more look at this golden rule, and you will find that scripture requires you to love yourself and have compassion for yourself no less than for your neighbor. Self hatred is surely as destructive and blasphemous as the hatred of others. For you too bear God's essence and you need to develop an awareness of your own sacred worth. Let me give you a personal gift of one of my favorite gems Rabbi Joshua ben Levi taught: wherever you may go, a retinue of angels precedes you and calls out, "Make way for the essence of the Holy One Blessed Be He." I can't think of a healthier self image to carry with you constantly. Should you be prone to self denigration or be excessively hard on yourself, it will help you forgive yourself and get on with the business of fulfilling your divine potential. On the other hand, if you tend toward egocentric self idolatry, it can move you to achieve a more realistic balance in self perception – to know that you are but one of billions of people equally sacred and precious to God.

> *He who knows others has knowledge.*
> *He who knows himself is illuminated.*
> Roshe

He who knows other men is discerning; he who knows himself is intelligent. He who overcomes others is strong; he who overcomes himself is mighty. Tao Teh King

"As God fills the world, so the human soul fills the body; as He sees all things but is visible to none, so the soul sees but cannot be seen. As He guides the world, so does the soul guide the body. As the Holy One is pure, so the soul is pure. As He dwells mystically within, so too does the soul."

Across all boundaries of time, cultures, religions and philosophies, the divine essence in us has been identified classically with our soul. That mystic intuition is a universal assumption for which there is no shred of objective evidence and there may never be. Here we re-encounter some premises of the Pardes theory — that methods of validation in one dimension may be irrelevant to another and that reality is much larger than our limited disciplines.

What is a greater mystery than life itself? We can describe some of its genetic components and biophysical processes. But who can quantify life's elan or isolate a spark of consciousness? In this dimension, intuitive experience and symbolism are appropriate modes of communication.

The sage of Proverbs wrote: "A human soul is the candle of God." His well known metaphor of the soul regards it as a spark out of the infinite flame that kindles all life.

A scholar, noted for his eloquence, was invited to address the graduation of an elementary Hebrew academy in Brooklyn. It was the final day of Chanukah and the speaker, transported to an ecstatic crescendo, cried out: "You yeshiva graduates, your souls are as sacred as these Chanukah candles. Long may you burn!" (Humor presents itself in so many unlikely circumstances.)

How do we understand the soul? The Kabbalistic

masters probed deeply into its nature. They searched metaphysically for what seems impenetrable to sensory experience — the mysterious source of our vitality, our potentiality, our creativity.

Like Gaul, they held that the soul was divided into three parts. The first is called Nefesh which may best be rendered as anima; it is the vital force that animates us and gives us the sense of being alive. From nefesh we derive the capacity to experience physical reality in all its dazzling splendor and subtlety. That element of the soul is in closest association with our body and its senses. It stimulates our creative power in refashioning the physical world, olam ha-asiya.

The second region of the soul, Ruah, is the source of our ethical awareness, our moral ability to distinguish between good and evil. All desires, both worthy and unworthy, spring from ruah. It provides the creative force that nourishes moral growth and the realization of moral potentiality. Our ethical choices in judgment and deed, whether life affirming or life negating, emerge out of this second area of the soul that functions in olam hayetzira, (the world of creative form).

Neshamah, the third and final dimension of the soul is pure spirit, pure intelligence, pure thought. It flows out of the infinite reservoir of divine wisdom and endows us with the most precious, mystical gift of all — a miraculous stream of ideas, thoughts, imaginings, abstract concepts and theories. The quintessence of our soul, neshama, relates us to the supreme realm of God's being, olam habriah, (the world of creative ideas).

Please beware of a linear tendency to picture these aspects of the soul as discrete areas. In Kabbalah, they are spiritually integrated and transcend all physical spatial models. Even as the Creator unites all the powers of His sefirot (emanations) in the unending processes of universal creation, so does the human soul function as a spiritual unity of dynamic energies enabling us to deal creatively with the many physical, moral and intellectual challenges of life on earth. This analogy is central to Kabbalistic thought on the mystique of the soul in human divine relations. I will comment on one of the more arresting issues suggested here: what light is shed by this conception of the soul upon our potentialities and our freedom to fulfill them?

God in Kabbalah is most frequently called En Sof, The Infinite One. If every human soul shares directly in His infinite essence, lt follows that each of us is endowed with many untapped latencies waiting to be realized in all four dimensions — physical-intellectual, esthetic, ethical and spiritual. Psychologists have been guessing for some time about how much of our potential we realize in the course of our lives. The best consensus estimates that most people live out their years with no more than five to ten percent of their latent capacities actualized. Should this guess be anywhere near the truth, the growth potential for all of us would have to be mind boggling!

"The greatness of one's soul is in direct proportion to the breadth of our vision and intent," wrote a master of Kabbalah. But is that really so? Does our intent have any relevance at all or is free will one of our grand illusions, as the old behaviorists and the new breed of psychobiologists keep telling us? Their view of human behavior as shaped entirely by genetic heritage and environmental influence — and therefore, predictable — is the latest formulation of a very old idea in history: that human beings are not free but shackled to some predetermined fate. Traces of this notion pervade the karmic symbolism of Indian theosophy, the astrological systems of ancient Babylon and Egypt that tie our destiny to the inexorable movement of stars and planets, the Greek

157

myth of the Fates and the Christian dogma of predestined grace.

All share in diminishing or eliminating our range of free will in the cultivation of our potential. A talented medieval poet-scholar, who was also a hopeless schlemiel (loser in the practical world), laughed at his own destiny in these lines:

"Were I a candlemaker, the sun would never set — If a trader in shrouds, no one would ever die."

The scriptural drama of human creation, however, focuses upon our freedom to make choices between goodness and evil, truth and falsehood, beauty and ugliness, sanctity and savagery of spirit. That too is an essence of God in us. Our freedom is, of course, not unlimited. We are surely circumscribed by physical inheritance, natural milieu and possibly other influences, but not mechanically predictable. There is an x-factor of human variability built into our system. It derives from the soul quickened by a spark of divine freedom. In an exquisite epigram of irreconcilable contradiction, the Ethics of the Fathers taught: "Everything is forseen by God but human freedom is granted."

Somewhere between the extremes of limitless free will and servile determinism lies the way of human responsibility and growth. Talmudic sages observed long ago that irresponsibility is the option of slaves. If we cannot take responsibility for our lives, if our thoughts and actions are nothing more than conditioned responses to prerecorded signals from biogenetic and environmental programming, what meaning is there to human dignity or hope?

You may not go so far as Maimonides who argued that every person is capable of achieving the righteousness of Moses or the wickedness of Jereboam. But then again, why not? We are so obsessed these days with the fathomless depths of the demonic in people. Why should we set arbitrary limits upon our capacity to become human?

Even as God is wise, gracious and compassionate, the ancients taught, so should we cultivate wisdom, graciousness and compassion. All of this would be quite pointless if we were not free to do so. Nobody expects kindness from a computer. Or should we? A recent story hailed the creation of a supercomputer, the apotheosis of computer science, programmed to handle every problem put to it. With some trepidation its operator posed the ultimate question

~ Is there a God?

The computer responded at once

~ There is now!

"Nothing we ever imagined
is beyond our power
Only beyond our present
self-knowledge."
Theodore Rozak

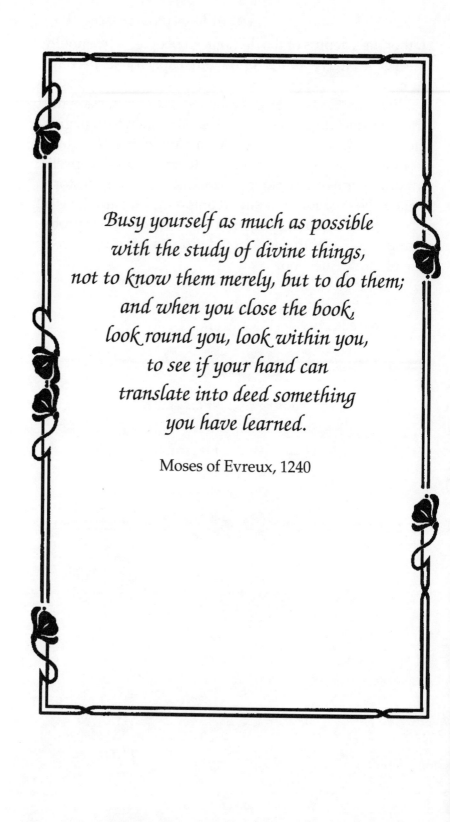

Busy yourself as much as possible
with the study of divine things,
not to know them merely, but to do them;
and when you close the book,
look round you, look within you,
to see if your hand can
translate into deed something
you have learned.

Moses of Evreux, 1240

BOOK FOUR

*Paradise on Earth
In Four Dimensions*

1. Toward a Philosophy of Life

GENESIS 6:9, 11-13, 17-19

"Noah was a righteous man unblemished in his age. . .but the earth was corrupt before God, it was filled with violence. And God saw how depraved the world had become for all flesh had perverted its way on earth. Then God said to Noah, 'The end has come for all living creatures before Me because the earth is filled with their violence. . .And I am about to bring on the deluge of waters upon the earth to eliminate all flesh under the sky having the breath of life; everything on earth will perish. But with you I am going to establish My covenant and you will enter the ark — you, your sons, your wife and your sons' wives. And of all living creatures, you will take two of each into the ark that they may survive with you — they are to be male and female."

PSHAT — DIMENSION OF OBJECTIVE MEANING

A pastor invited his flock to gather on the sabbath and hear his sermon on "The Catastrophic Flood." In a few days, he received several letters of response from his congregants, all of them conveying regrets for not attending but they did enclose a check for the flood victims.

This flood epic is surely among the best known biblical stories. It has also spawned a delightful folk humor of which the following is a worthy example. One famous skeptic opined that, of all the many problems he

162

had with the tale of Noah, what he found most difficult to believe was this: that no more than two asses were on board the ark!

Modern archeology is indispensable to us in our search for an objective, historical understanding of the unforgettable Noah saga. Was it unique to biblical literature? In a thematic sense, no; in its creative treatment, yes.

During the years 1849-1854, a historic archaeological expedition unearthed thousands of tablets and fragments from the buried library of King Ashurbanipal, who reigned in Nineveh, capital of the great Assyrian Empire, more than 2,650 years ago. Among the treasures recovered there was the Epic of Gilgamesh, one of the masterpieces of ancient near eastern literature. Its eleventh tablet holds particular significance for us in that it contains a poetic account of some terrible deluge in the world of antiquity, which is strikingly similar in several factual details to our scriptural flood story.

Subsequent finds have dug up many fragmented copies of this epic poem all over southwest Asia, including Israel, Anatolia and Turkey. Its primary antecedents, we now know, go back to Sumerian originals more than 4,000 years ago and its popular influence extended even to Greece. Undoubtedly the biblical editors of our Noahite Flood narrative were acquainted with Gilgamesh and used some of its well known data, which had long become part of the general culture.

Both stories, for example, describe a hero who was saved from a disastrous flood, our biblical Noah and the Babylonian Utnapishtim. Both heroes were instructed to build a boat to specifications. Both survived a flood that inundated all life and their boats came to rest upon a mountain (Mt. Ararat for Noah — Mt. Nisir for Utnapishtim). Again both of them sent out a raven and a dove (Utnapishtim adds a swallow) to determine the safe time for disembarking and finally, they both offered sacrifices of thanksgiving upon their deliverance.

But if the similarities between scriptural and Mesopotamian deluge traditions are interesting, the contrasts between them are even more significant. You may recall our previous comparison of the creation account in the Bible with other cosmogenic myths in the culture at large. We found that it is not what Scripture accepts from the surrounding culture but what it rejects that gives us a deeper grasp of its authentic message. The same is true here.

I am not referring to petty dissimilarities of fact, like those about the number and choice of passengers aboard Noah's ark and Utnapishtim's boat, or the duration of the deluge, or the sequence of birds dispatched by each, and many others. The really important differences between the biblical flood account on the one hand and that of Gilgamesh and all other Mesopotamian versions on the other, touch upon the most fundamental issues of religion and ethics.

What we have here is a radical step forward in ancient ideas about God and society. To grasp it, we need to answer the question: how does the literal intent of the biblical flood epic contrast with that of all other known deluge myths in the ancient near east?

The Gilgamesh classic gives no reason or motive for the gods' decision to wipe out human life; the reader is left to assume that it was all a capricious whim of the divine assembly. Another version of the deluge myth is presented by the Atrahasis epic that has come down to us in Babylonian and Assyrian fragments. It tells us how the god Enlil complained to the assembled gods that people had become too numerous on earth and so noisy as to disturb the gods' sleep. Presumably the flood was to solve that little problem. One shudders to think of

how they might have reacted to the typical, high deci-
bel, mass punk rock concerts of today!

And if the catastrophe itself was inflicted upon humankind with no apparent justification or meaning, so
the surviving hero makes it only by a stroke of good
luck. Utnapishtim is saved from the flood for no other
reason than his being a favorite of the god Ea. When
Enlil, "wisest of gods," learns that his plan for total
genocide had thus been frustrated,

> *"He was filled with wrath. . .*
> *Has some living soul escaped?*
> *No man was to survive the destruction!"*

The Bible repudiated this ancient world view of divine caprice and its corollary, the futility and
meaninglessness of human life. It was an historic break,
a total rejection of amoral polytheism, social instability
and individual despair. And the creative achievement of
our scriptural flood epic was the fruit of that rejection...
as well as the conduit to a new affirmation.

What are some of these new ideas being asserted and
new values affirmed? You will not find them listed theoretically; that was not the current literary style. They
emerge by direct inference from the narrative itself.

Clearly the thrust of our biblical flood story is its
complete moral reshaping of old deluge memories. To
such a point had the scriptural concept of ethical monotheism progressed that the notion of destroying the whole
human race for no reason at all — or for its loud interfer-
ence with divine sleep — was now altogether repugnant.
Over and over again we are informed that the whole
society of Noah's contemporaries was corrupt, filled with
injustice, violence and crime. What is more, Noah was
not saved by any divine favoritism but because he alone
was found to be righteous in his generation.

A fundamental assumption of scripture is that to

violate moral law is to endanger human survival even as the undermining of nature's law could destroy our planet. This literal motif of the biblical flood story may have seemed avant-garde for its time but today all of us confront its full challenge. Will the violent explosion of crime, terror and brutality in our generation set off the final thermonuclear deluge for all life on earth?

A scriptural prophet said it well: "As I live, saith the Lord, I take no pleasure in the death of the corrupt but that he rechannel his way and live."

I will not conclude this section without a word on the one question everybody asks sooner or later about this story. Is it historically true? Did the flood ever occur in fact? Our best answer is that all the evidence is not yet in. We are dealing, after all, with prerecorded history. However, some geological studies of the Mesopotamian plains bear evidence of heavy inundations that once submerged large areas of the lower Tigris Euphrates valley in ancient times. Archaeological excavations confirm the existence of clay deposits from substantial flood levels in the area.

But the most impressive testimony of all is given by the flood of deluge myths themselves. Historians have learned to take them seriously, as the collective memory of prehistoric peoples, who transmitted them orally long before committing them to written records. The many related flood stories of ancient Mesopotamia, including our biblical account, presuppose the tragic occurrence of an awesome deluge, which left indelible and traumatic imprints upon the consciousness of many peoples.

DIMENSION OF ALLEGORY— REMEZ

Too bad the Bible has fallen into the hands of so many joyless, prunefaced proponents. Who nowadays turns to its pages for humor? Or even recognizes scriptural wit in the forbidding translations that entomb it? The Hebrew poet laureate of this century, Chaim Nachman Bialik, used to say that reading the Bible in translation is like kissing your beloved through a handkerchief — it does not have the same flavor.

You will be surprised to encounter an exquisite piece of satire at the end of the Noah epic. Most readers miss it completely; even scholars, or should I say, especially scholars pass it by. It's all in one simple line that blends an anticlimax of unrivalled power with a parable of timeless vitality. The best ending of O. Henry pales before it.

This story is not concluded, as is generally thought, when the waters recede and Noah comes out of the ark to offer a sacrifice to God and receive His blessing. A postscript was added, a masterful one liner, which is the true finale. Let me explain.

Who among us have not dreamed at least once in our lives about how different things would be, if we had the power to fashion a new world? We would build a paradisiac society, not like those miserable politicians who have brought our world to such a sorry state. Well Noah had that unrepeatable chance. For him the fantasy was realized in full...a brave new world, all his to shape from scratch.

How did he confront that grand challenge? "And Noah, man of the soil, started planting a vineyard; he drank of the wine, got himself drunk and wallowed naked in his tent!" The curtain falls and the tale is ended.

A sharp satire of Noah, that "righteous man," in a surprise anticlimax of genius — Noah copped out! The challenge was too big for him. Overwhelmed by it all, he withdraws to his tent for the perfect escape. There he lies farshnushket! (hopelessly inebriated)

And even here the consummate art of this finale is not exhausted. Woven into its fabric is a parable that never loses its vigor. Noah symbolizes you and me. We too are given the chance to fashion a new world, the miniature universe that is every human being. And how do we meet that challenge? Like Noah, we all have our copouts, our favorite addictions to drink, drugs, food, work, television, gambling, pornography, acquisitiveness, withdrawal, depression, cultism. . .the modes of escape are subtle and legion. Inexorably the years run out for us and for our world of latencies that were never developed. We play a witless game with our lives and the joke is on us.

Let me add to this formidable allegory the spice of an ancient legend told by the sages about Noah's vineyard. It seems that when he began to work the vines, Satan came by and asked

~ What are you planting?
~ A vineyard, said Noah.
~ What sort of product will it grow?
~ Sweet fruits, both moist and dry, out of which we produce wine that gladdens the heart.
~How about a partnership with me on this vineyard?
~ Sure.

What did Satan do?— He took a lamb and slaughtered it over the vine, after which he did the same with a lion, a monkey and a pig.

Then he explained these symbolic acts to Noah. When a person drinks the first cup down, he is like a lamb, humble and of contrite spirit. The second cup gives him the illusion of being powerful as a lion and he becomes arrogant "I'm the greatest!" After tippling three or four cups, he behaves like a monkey — gets up, dances, giggles and befouls his mouth publicly, all the while unaware of what's going on. Stone drunk, he is degraded to the level of a swine, rolling in slop and reveling in the dung.

Does the Bible lay a backhanded compliment on Noah? The classic medieval commentator, Rashi, quotes older sources that differ on this issue. In discussing our verse, "Noah was a righteous man in his generation," Rashi explains: "Some of our sages consider this scripture a fine tribute to Noah. If he could lead a righteous life in a corrupt generation, how much more so in a generation of saints." Others, however, feel that we have here the faint praise of a Jewish compliment. "Sure, in the company of scoundrels, Noah stands out as a righteous man but if he lived in the generation of Abraham, he wouldn't have amounted to much."

Why are Jews so hard on their heroes? Noah's counterpart in the Gilgamesh epic, Utnapishtim, is deified after the deluge. Nowhere is it claimed that he made it because of any ethical virtue on his part, but only by divine favoritism. Noah, on the other hand, was spared clearly because of his ethical lifestyle. And what happens to him? Not only is he denied deification but they're still debating to this day the extent of his righteousness.

Which reminds me of an authentic folk story about a little town in Soviet Russia three centuries ago. In his opulent palace, the local Count was celebrating his birthday attended by all the nobility of the area. It was traditionally a week long binge and by now most of the guests were pie-eyed to the point of boredom. The rich and powerful host, desperate for a gimmick to liven up his party, remembered how Yossel the shamus sounded the shofar (ram's horn) at synagogue on the Jewish New Year, when it was proper for the Count to make his formal visit.

~Fetch Yossel and his shofar at once, he shouted to his lackeys.

169

Nobody messed around with an order from the Count. In a few minutes, Yossel was ushered into a huge, ornate reception hall and heard the Count bellow:

~ Yossel, blow that shofar like you never blew it before!

He put the horn to his lips and all the guests were roused out of their stupor. The sound was new and mysterious. They began to throw gold coins to the old man, who had known only the most abject poverty all his life. Never had he seen so much gold; it was a miracle. Quickly he stuffed every pocket with gold coins and ran breathless all the way home.

~ Sarah, he cried out to his aged spouse in their wretched mud hut, if you must blow the shofar, better blow it for the gentiles rather than the Jews!

Applying that line to our discussion of Noah, one might conclude: if you plan to be a hero, better be a hero for the non-Jews rather than the Jews. But the fact is that a profound ethical truth is involved here that goes beyond heroics.

There is a serious flaw in Noah's righteousness (Noah is, of course, all of us) and the Kabbalistic teachers of Zohar illumine it well. When God revealed the impending flood to Noah and instructed him to build an ark for himself and his family, what did he do? Did he intercede for his fellow creatures to save them from annihilation? Did he plead for divine compassion? Did he do anything to help? Not a word, not a thing! Humanity is sentenced to death and Noah accepts it, satisfied that he and his are to be spared.

Not so with Abraham. When he was informed that his enemies, the people of Sodom and Gemorrah had been sentenced to death for the same violent crimes of Noah's generation, he pleads their case aggressively before God. "Will you destroy the righteous with the

wicked? Will the Judge of the world Himself act unjustly? Abraham's moral concern is not confined to his
immediate family; it embraces the whole human family.

Let's be fair to Noah. At least he cared for his family,
an instinct humans share with many other living species. How do you deal with the runaway lifestyle of
"Take-Care-Of-Number-One," currently being marketed
as self-awareness? That neat euphemism for egomania
makes it quite kosher to relieve yourself of personal
concern even for your own family. Who then but a hopeless masochist will care for the communal, national and
global family?

The ethical neo-primitivism of our age confronts us
with much more than a trauma of embarrassment. Whatever hope we can sustain for our survival hinges directly
upon our success in bridging the deadly gap between
our remarkably advanced technology and our incred-
ibly retarded morality. Nothing short of a revolution of
wisdom will get us into the twenty-first century!

Reverence for life is where religion and philosophy can meet and where society must try to go.

Norman
Cousins

THE MYSTICAL DIMENSION — SOD

Who was Noah's wife and why is her name not even
mentioned in scripture? From time immemorial, that
mystery has remained unsolved. One ancient sage suggested she was Naamah, sister of Tubal-Cain, but his
contemporaries.disagreed. The Bible is silent, a fact which
feminists and humorists have been confronting lately in
different ways.

One wit took off on a midrashic story that tells how
Noah spent 120 years building the ark.

Passersby would ask:

~ What are you doing there Noah?

~ Building an ark.

~ A what?

~ An ark. You see, the Lord is going to unleash a huge flood all over the earth because everybody's been so wicked. And He commanded me to build this ark in order to save myself and my family. You can be saved too, if you change your ways. And they would laugh at him.

~ Poor old Noah has gone crackers.

Even his wife would taunt him relentlessly.

~ Look at that shlemiel I got for a husband. Every man is out there making money for his wife and children but what is he doing? He's building an ark, that's what.

Finally the ark was completed. Noah's family and all the animals, birds and reptiles were safe inside. When the terrible deluge began, Noah turned to his wife

~ Now honey, aren't you glad I built this ark?

~ Thanks for nothing.

~ What's the matter now?

~ Listen here, did you get a whiff of that zoo you shlept on board? Who do you think is going to clean up all that mess?

Well, not every mystery can be solved but some can at least be enjoyed.

As a striking illustration of how the mystical dimension of biblical exegesis can yield invaluable wisdom, I have chosen a comment by the Zohar on our Noah epic. Scripture states: "And the Lord saw how the earth had been ruined." This would indicate that Noah's generation had devastated nature as well as society. With mindless greed and a coarseness of spirit, they had so polluted and wasted the earth that it now lay enfeebled, a helpless victim to the raging floodwaters.

Of all living species, according to Genesis, humans alone were invested with managerial authority and the power to use it. You will recall that Adam, Eve and their descendants were mandated to govern our planet. Intrinsic to that mandate was the conviction that we were qualified to do the job; that we were designed to be co-creators with God—to learn, to organize, to invent, to search, to discover, to build, to conserve, to produce, to share and to pursue truth, beauty and goodness. Every personal deed, the Kabbalists teach, in fulfillment of that sacred design for human life draws God's presence (Shekhinah) closer to us on earth, blessing us with joy, abundance and well-being.

But we have persistently mismanaged our planet. To this day we plunder, exploit, degrade, oppress, violate and destroy it, choosing to distort truth, befoul beauty and pervert goodness. In so doing, we drive the Shekhinah into exile, a separation bringing us much misery, dysphoria and anomie.

With this symbolism, the Zohar illumines our full range of power and the consequences attending both to its use and abuse. Where can we experience true fulness of joy more directly than in the sacred union between a lover and his beloved? Conversely, when do we feel the depressiveness of sorrow more bitterly than in separation, estrangement and isolation from one another?

Once you accept the premise that we humans are an integral part of the divine process, then our efficacy and challenge become enormous. Not only can we advance the reconciliation of people to one another; the re-integration of society and nature; the rapprochement between human beings and the Shekhinah; but also the reunion between the Infinite God and His Shekhinah (the Sovereign and His Bride). That human beings have a meaningful role in the harmonious re-unification of the inner Godhood is one of the boldest visions within Kabbalah. It inspired a permanent addition to Hasidic liturgy: before the performance of a mitzvah (a religious or ethical deed) and the blessing that accompanies it, the individual recites, "For the sake of the union of the Holy

173

One Blessed Be He and His Shekhinah." Doing the mitzvah in performance of God's will is what confers cosmic potency upon us. It is a power for the triumph of joy and love.

Noah's generation had abused that power. That is how the Zohar understands our biblical verse: "And God saw how the earth had been ruined for all flesh had perverted its way on earth." People then chose, not a world of unity, of drawing closer to one another, to nature and to God, but a world of fragmentation, self-centered, self-serving estrangement, a joyless age of estrangement, self-idolatry, violence and total destruction.

This problem of perverting human power, which the mystics find underlying the classic flood epic in scripture, is still the core issue of our day. What kind of a world do we want to live in? A world of xenophobic violence, of atavistic terror? Of growing alienation and internecine hostility? Of hopeless misery, suffering and extinction? That's exactly what we're rushing mindlessly into. Our diminishing joy, expanding stress and pervasive despair are the signposts telling us how far we have come on this deadend road.

Noah was given a second chance. A new creation was ushered in after the flood, a new start for life on earth and even a new covenant established between God and humankind.

Before we in the twentieth century pass the point of no return, the Kabbalists are telling us here to give ourselves a second chance, to redirect our lives and rechannel our energies into alma diyichuda, a world of healing, hope and happiness.

Why was humanity granted a second chance in the days of Noah? A perceptive biblical verse informs us that, "the inclination of man's heart is destructive because of his youth." This excuse of the relative youth of our species on earth had some validity during Noah's primitive age of prehistory; it is irrelevant to us today. What is more, our sophisticated, technical instruments for the liquidation of all planetary life simply rule out any possibility of a second chance. If we're ever going to exercise our life-affirming options the time is now!

The Hebrew term Shalom, generally interpreted as peace, means more than just the cessation of hostility and violence. It is a positive state, meant to convey a kind of inner as well as outer tranquility. I think of it as a state in which the heart is totally at ease.

Below are some other thoughts on peace:

Peace is not absence of war, it is a virtue, a state of mind, a disposition for benevolence, confidence, justice. Benedict Spiniza

The "price of peace" can never reach such dimensions to equal the smallest fraction of war's deadly cost. Ambassador Abba Eban

What we now need to discover in the social realm is the moral equivalent of war: something heroic that will speak to men as universally as war does, and yet will be as compatible to their spiritual selves as war has proved itself to be incompatible. William James

It is safe to say that no farmer ever got a corn crop by simply reassuring himself periodically, "I'm not going to let my land grow up in weeds!" Similarly, the people of the world can never hope to reap the benefits of permanent peace by reassuring themselves daily, "We will have no more war." Just as there is no corn crop without planting and cultivation, so there will be no growth toward peace without the planting and cultivation of attitudes that breed peace. Helen L. Toner

Men must be able to find in peacetime pursuits, the same satisfaction, the same opportunity for sacrifice, the same outlet for idealistic emotion as, till now, only war has been able to provide them. James Bryan

Peace cannot be kept by force, it can only be achieved by understanding. Albert Einstein

2. On Self-fulfillment And Social Renewal

Genesis 12: 1-3

And God said to Abraham: Go forth from your native land and from your father's home to a land that I will show you. And I will make of you a great nation, I will bless you and cause your name to be exalted. . .and through you, all families on earth shall be blessed.

DIMENSION OF OBJECTIVE MEANING — PSHAT

ot a word about Abraham's childhood is mentioned in the Bible. But the midrash preserved this delightful story. Terah, Abraham's father, was an idolmaker by trade. One day he went out and asked the lad to take over. By the time he returned, every idol had been smashed except for the biggest one, which was holding a huge rod in its hands. Enraged, Terah shouted,

~ Who did this?

~ How can I withold anything from you, answered Abraham. A woman came here carrying a platter of meal and told me to offer it to the gods. I did so and suddenly a quarrel broke out among them. Each god demanded the right to eat first until that big one grabbed hold of a rod and hacked all the others to pieces.

~ Are you trying to make a fool out of me? They're only idols; what do they know?

176

~ Quite so, father, won't you please listen to what you yourself have said?

This tale reinforced an old folk memory about one of the chief iconoclasts of all time. Abraham belongs to that rare company of individuals who made irrevocable changes in the course of history. He had the courage to break radically with the past and chart a new course for the future.

Something very important needs to be said here. A polaric change has taken place in our historical understanding of Abraham and the whole biblical process he initiated. Less than 60 years ago, before the spectacular archaeological finds at Mari, Nuzi, later at Ebla and elsewhere in the Middle East, most biblical scholars were treating the Genesis stories about Abraham as legendary folklore. "We attain to no historical knowledge of the patriarchs but only of the time when the stories about them arose in the Israelite people," asserted the ranking authority on biblical criticism a century ago. His judgment was accepted rapidly by "higher biblical critics" with a unanimous enthusiasm reminiscent of the Marxist faithful receiving party doctrine.

All that has changed dramatically. We now have objective evidence from primary sources about the social, political and cultural life of the biblical world during the patriarchal age. All scholars today are impressed with its strong external support for the scriptural traditions concerning Abraham and his descendents.

Yet nothing within the Bible or outside of it prepares us for his sudden call: "Go forth. . ." A strange journey Abraham feels summoned to make, to abandon his ancestral home and country for "a land which I will show you". The land is not even named. . .and appropriately so. What was destined to become the Land of Israel was then, some 4,000 years ago, a minor outpost, a buffer and bridge between the major empires of the Tigris Euphrates and the Nile.

It was Abraham's spiritual quest in this tiny, peripheral land that began to transform it into the Holy Land. On this soil he and his children created sacred history and from its borders, the monotheistic vision and faith — spanning the whole biblical enterprise — went out to inspire the world.

It takes guts to follow the call, "Lech Lecha — Go forth!" Abraham was turning his back on the leading civilization of his day, giving up a comfortable life in his native Mesopotamia at the height of its political power, wealth, intellectual and social progress. For what? To pursue his vision in no man's land, a stranger in rugged terrain, always on the move, living in tents, never settling down permanently.

He stakes his life on the truth of his vision, a new integrating faith in one God and one human family — a vision to invest life with enduring value and hope, and a faith to encourage the growth of all people. Only when he takes that risk, says his final goodbyes and moves on to the next stage of his life's work, does he emerge out of obscurity to achieve a blessing for himself and for all families on earth.

That challenge to "go forth" was perceived by tradition as Abraham's first test of faith and mettle. In the simple comment of Rashi, the classic expositor of Pshat, it was a summons "to his own well-being and fulfillment".

We are not all history making visionaries like Abraham. Yet this call to personal growth in its most literal sense does confront everyone of us. What is more gauche than the sight of aged men and women hanging on pitifully to their long lost youth, terrorized to move on to the next stage of their lives? Of a famous, former film star well past his prime, one of Hollywood's most caustic wits remarked: "He's very loyal. Years ago, he reached an age he liked and stayed with it."

How many people store up whole lifetimes of frustration and misery by standing pat in their cocoons of the mind, heart and spirit? They hear the call to go forth but they can't quite muster the courage to take a risk and venture beyond the comfortable borders of their past. These are society's losers, a lost blessing to themselves and to others.

Israel Baal Shem Tov, founder of modern Hasidism, interpreted a classic Hebrew prayer in this light. Why, he asked, do we recite in our prayers, "God of Abraham, God of Isaac and God of Jacob?" Why not simply God of Abraham, Isaac and Jacob? Because Isaac and Jacob did not limit themselves to Abraham's experience in searching for God. They pursued their own quests and developed their own ways of divine service.

That call to go forward is with us all our lives. Moses heard it as a young prince in Pharaoh's court and he abandoned la vita dolce of unimaginable luxury to help his enslaved brothers. At the age of 80, he was summoned again from a pastoral retirement in Midian to start a new career as liberator of his people. Wherever you are in your life cycle, you can achieve blessing for yourself and for others. Go forth!

Whatever you can do or dream, you can begin it...
Boldness has genius, power and magic in it!
Goethe

Three major world religions trace their origins to Abraham: Judaism through the birthright of Isaac and Jacob; Islam via the lineage of Ishmael and Christianity by a spiritual patrimony of faith. This striking fact of history and its benign possibilities for the whole human enterprise is wrapped up allegorically in the scriptural promise to the patriarch: "and through you, all families on earth shall be blessed."

Logically and theologically, you might have expected that these religions would have drawn closer to one another over the years and learned to cherish each other through their kinship of sharing in a common ethico-spiritual legacy. The insane truth, however, is that they have interrelated, not out of kinship or love, but with violent hostility. In betrayal of everything Abraham represented, they practiced injustice, hatred, oppression, ghettoization, pogrom, massacre, torture and burning at the stake — Christians against Moslems, Moslems against Christians and both against Jews. Nor was this savage persecution limited to non-believers outside the ranks of the faithful; dissidents from within were also made to suffer the most cruel affliction.

That deadly antagonism between religions is reflected in a classic of folk humor. Three clergymen — a priest, a minister and a rabbi — finished their earthly careers on the same day and were greeted on high by the angel Gabriel, who said

~ Our custom here is to grant one wish to every righteous man before assigning him to his place in heaven. Father, what is your wish?

~ I must confess that my lifelong wish has been to witness the downfall of the whole Protestant heresy.

~ That's a radical wish requiring the judgment of the heavenly tribunal, said Gabriel. Please have a seat while you're waiting. And you, Reverand, what is your wish?

~ My prayerful hope for many years has been to see the destruction of the Roman Church and its papacy.

~ That too is beyond my jurisdiction. You will also have to wait for the heavenly tribunal's decision. And you, Rabbi, do you have a special wish?

~ I'm not in a hurry, said the rabbi, please take care of my two colleagues first.

When you think about it, it's tragic enough that such enmity existed in the past but the persistence of religious armed conflict into the closing decades of the Twentieth Century is utterly obscene. Isaiah wrote:

"Look to the rock from which you were hewn
And explore deeply the source from which you were dug.
Look to Abraham, your father and to
Sarah who gave birth to you."

Abraham's calling, his life's work was to go forth and serve as a blessing for all people, to fill his days with acts of justice, hospitality and loving kindness. . .to create a lifestyle validating his belief in one God and one human family. An ancient sage taught: "All who act compassionately to their fellow human beings are surely authentic children of Abraham, our father, but those who have no compassion upon people are in no way his descendents."

I hereby issue this public proposal to the world leaders of Judaism, Islam and Christianity, all who claim authentic lineage from Abraham. The time is long overdue for the calling of a world Religious Summit to gather together with the leaders of all other great religious traditions, such as Buddhism, Hinduism and others. Its purpose is to end this curse of religious, racial and ethnic xenophobia and to lay the foundations for a new era of universal blessing.

181

THE FOUR DIMENSIONS OF PARADISE

That Summit agenda must address itself to the immediate end of all religious armed conflct, such as:

1. Terrorism and bloodshed between Catholics and Protestants in Northern Ireland.
2. The hostility between Suunite and Shiite Moslems, which has erupted into a full-scale war between Iraq and Iran.
3. The malignant spread of Jew hatred around the world; the most vicious export centers for this new anti-Jewish propaganda are the former Soviet Union and fanatic sources in some Islamic states.
4. The bitter, violent enmity between Hindus and Moslems all over the Far East.
5. An end to religious bigotry and intolerance every where.
6. An end to ecclesiastic imperialism which arrogates to itself an institutional monopoly over access to God in this world and an exclusive franchise upon His salvation to all eternity. Of all the totalitarian arrogance threatening us today, nothing is more spiritually repulsive than religious chauvinism.

Out of that Summit should come a world wide commitment:
1. To religious democracy in spirit and in action.
2. To religious freedom, dignity, equality and respect for everyone. The scriptural prophet, Micah, said it best: "For all peoples may walk, each one in the name of his divinity and we will go forth in the name of the Lord, our God forever."
3. To teach, inspire and serve rather than dominate or coerce people on issues of spiritual faith and religious lifestyle.

A very ancient story clarifies this last commitment

182

admirably. Abraham was known in the Holy Land of antiquity for his open and generous hospitality. Travelers in the Negev wilderness would stop by his tent every day and everyone was welcomed warmly and treated to good food, drink and lodging. After dining to their heart's content, they would start to thank their host but he would always interrupt them, saying:

~ Why do you thank me? Is anything here mine? Let us both thank the one Creator of the Universe Who has blessed us both with His abundance.

And so, all of Abraham's guests would learn to recite the blessings of grace and their hearts would be turned to God.

One evening, a very old man came in off the desert. After dining, when Abraham suggested that his guest give thanks not to him but to God, he refused, denying the existence of any divinity and holding all such beliefs in contempt. Even Abraham lost his temper and ordered the old man to leave. When he was gone, God came to Abraham and said:

~ Abraham, Abraham, I suffered that atheist for eighty years and you could not tolerate him for one night?

DIMENSION OF ETHIC — DERASHA

What moral sense is there to Abraham's blessing: "And I shall make of you a great nation?" Nations are not perceived nowadays as instruments of blessing. Thorstein Veblin wrote: "The nation, being in effect a licensed predatory concern, is not bound by the decencies of that code of laws and morals that governs private conduct." Einstein was more succinct: "Nationalism is an infantile disease. . .the measles of mankind."

From earliest recorded time, national glory has been measured by military conquest, the expansion of territorial borders, the accumulation of political-economic power and the subjugation, the exploitation of people. Here a new concept of national purpose is proposed; it becomes a core concept in Abraham's religious-ethical-social revolution. "I will make of you a great nation," so that "all families on earth may be blessed in you."

This new experiment in national community would no longer measure a country's worth by the size of its territory, population, gross national product or military power. " By justice shall a nation become great." Not domination but service was to be the future gage of national fulfillment.

I submit that the enfolding of this new idea of nation-hood became a major theme of the whole Hebrew Bible. Both the first and second states of Israel were small nations, limited in natural resources and modest in military power. Yet they managed to achieve a greatness in history, paradigmatic and enduring. Many peoples in the most remote areas of our planet to this day know the biblical history of Israel better than their own. Why? Because it sought for the first time to define the goals of nationhood in ethical terms: the pursuit of justice, compassion and peace. Despite its many failures and shortcomings, none of them whitewashed but honestly recorded in scripture (quite uncommon among national literatures from antiquity to recent times), the first 2,000 years of Jewish history are still studied today as sacred history.

What Abraham started was enlarged and refined by the genius of Israel's prophets: "Man will not prevail by force. . ." "Not by military strength, nor by power but by my spirit, saith the Lord".

The midrash tells an unforgettable legend about the Macedonian conqueror, Alexander the Great. During his victorious campaign in Asia, he came to an unknown

184

kingdom and asked the king about its laws and customs. As they were sitting together, two litigants were brought before the king to plead their case. The first one said:

~ Your majesty, I purchased a field from this man and, while ploughing it, I unearthed a great treasure. So I told him: take your treasure. I purchased the land, not the treasure.

Whereupon the second litigant responded

~ The field and everything in it, from the depths of the earth to the heights of the heavens, all of it I sold to you in good faith. The treasure is yours.

Then the king addressed the first man:

~ Do you have a son?

~ Yes.

~ And you, he said to the other one, do you have a daughter?

~ Yes.

~ Then let them both marry and this treasure will be their wedding gift.

Alexander was amazed. His royal host asked:

~ Don't you think well of my judgment?

~ Very well, indeed, said the Greek.

~ Tell me, how would you have adjudicated it in your country?

~ I would have beheaded them both and added the treasure to my royal coffers.

Hearing that, the Asiatic king asked:

~ Does the sun shine in Greece?

~ Yes.

~ And the rains fall?

~ Yes.

~ Are there small cattle, goats, lambs and sheep in your land?

~ Yes.

185

~ Then it must be the virtue of those blameless animals that brings the blessings of sun and rain to such a nation.

Go forth, Abraham and all of us are told, get out of this predator model of nationhood and move forward to a humane vision of national service. Should nations compete for international glory? Of course! The glory of who contributes more to the advancement of knowledge, the alleviation of human suffering, the enrichment of life and the achievement of peace. Were this in fact true, what a glorious world we could be living in!

Is anything more symptomatic of our contemporary neoprimitivism than the fact that this common sense biblical idea of national purpose still strikes us as utopian? Why? Because we have not yet emerged out of the most dangerous of all atavistic idolatries, the cult of the national state, which has usurped the divine power of unlimited sovereignty.

We have not taken seriously the wisdom of scripture in restricting all human sovereignty before the unlimited sovereignty of divine justice and compassion. Three thousand years ago, David said, "Yours alone is the sovereignty, O Lord, and You are exalted supreme above all." The poet of Psalms added: "Sovereignty belongs to God and He reigns over the nations." Under His sovereignty, "the heavens rejoice and the earth is glad, the sea and all its creatures exult uproarious; the meadows celebrate with all their living things while the trees of the forest sing in joy."

But when humans play god and arrogate for themselves unlimited sovereignty, the heavens are polluted and the earth is ravaged, the sea despoiled, the fields wasted and forests laid bare. All of nature and society is depressed into mourning by a state idolatry which leads inexorably to death. If nations continue to recognize no higher sanction than their own self-interest and no limitations upon their sovereign right to make war, how can we escape an apocalyptic end to the brief experiment of human life on this planet?

The more you consider Abraham's idea on the ethical mandate of nationhood, the more admirable, the more indispensable it becomes. Moses was the first to apply and codify it when he forged the nation of Israel out of an inchoate mass of liberated slaves. Only limited sovereignty was to be granted to the kings of Israel. They were held to be responsible for upholding the moral and spiritual laws of the Bible no less than any other Israelite. And when they violated those laws, as did Saul, David, Ahab and Jereboam among others, some of the greatest ethical-spiritual teachers of all time, the prophets Samuel, Nathan, Elijah, Amos, Isaiah, Micah, Jeremiah and others were not afraid to indict them publicly for their misdeeds.

Out of this tradition, enriched with Hellenistic ideas on political philosophy, the concept of parliamentary government evolved from the Magna Carta in thirteenth century England to the American Revolution. Its thrust was to control the unlimited sovereignty of national government. In our American system, an intricate network of constitutional checks and balances delimits the power of government to make it serve and not enslave the people.

But all around the earth these days, the clock is being turned back to state idolatry. Military dictatorships still dominate a major portion of the world's population. Most of them play the game of democracy; it's good propaganda to exhibit a public facade of parliamentary and constitutional structures, no matter how hollow or impotent, and periodically to honor them in stylized ritual. Few are deceived but all tremble before the unlimited terror of the false god, the totalitarian state party and its leader. And if that retrogression were not tragic

187

enough, we must also suffer the unmitigated chutzpah of hearing this neo-enslavement euphemized as freedom.

Not one but many nationalisms were sired by Abraham, as scripture foretold "No longer will you be called Abram; your name shall be Abraham for I will make you the father of many nations." Issuing from his son Isaac and his grandson Jacob (surnamed Israel), the first and second biblical states of Israel and now the modern, third State of Israel constitute a 4,000-year Jewish national legacy from "Abraham, our father."

Many Arab nations today also proclaim their lineage from Abraham through his son Ishmael. In the prevailing climate of violent conflct between Arab and Jewish nationalisms, who can find a trace of the blessing vouchsafed to Abraham? Only the clear lens of history can correct our myopic illusions, which sees the current hostility as endemic and hopeless. Even a cursory glance at centuries of Islamic-Jewish relations will show that all the fierce rancor today has been whipped up only during the past seven decades.

History has a way of upsetting our most securely reinforced opinions. Did you know, for example, that from the eighth to the fourteenth century while most of Europe was steeped in abysmal ignorance, Arabs and Jews in Spain, North Africa and the middle East created together a cultural renaissance unrivalled anywhere on earth? This rich cultural symbiosis took place within a remarkably open society, such as Moslem Spain, where a Jew could and did rise to the office of prime minister (vizir) in Granada during the eleventh century.

Nor do we have to go back to the middle ages. A twentieth century agreement of great warmth and friendship between the accredited world leaders of Arab nationalism and of the Zionist movement was worked out at the end of World War I. Here are some excerpts from the text of this enormously important document, which was signed in London on January 3, 1919, by the Emir Feisal ibn Hussein, the Sherif of Mecca and Dr. Chaim Weizmann, President of the World Zionist Organization:

"His Royal Highness the Emir Feisal, representing and acting on behalf of the Arab Kingdom of Hedjaz and Dr. Chaim Weitzmann, representing and acting on behalf of the Zionist Organization, mindful of the racial kinship and ancient bonds existing between the Arabs and the Jewish people, and realizing that the surest means of working out the consummation of their national aspirations is through the closest possible collaboration in the development of the Arab State and Palestine, and being desirous further of confirming the good understanding which exists between them, have agreed upon the following:

The Arab state and Palestine in all their relations and undertakings shall be controlled by the most cordial good will and understanding, and to this end Arab and Jewish duly accredited agents shall be established and maintained in the respective territories.

All necessary measures shall be taken to encourage and stimulate immigration of Jews into Palestine on a large scale, and as quickly as possible to settle Jewish immigrants upon the land through closer settlement and intensive cultivation of the soil. In taking such measures the Arab peasant and tenant farmers shall be assisted in forwarding their economic development."

Two months later on March 3, 1919, the Emir Feisal clarified the intent of this agreement in a letter to the famous American jurist, Felix Frankfurter, who was then in Paris, as head of the American Zionist delegation to the Peace Conference. The whole world — especially Palestinians, Israelis, Arabs and Jews today — all of us

189

need to rediscover this mind-boggling correspondence in order to redress the tragic mistakes of the past and renew the authentic good will and great hope expressed at that time.

Delegation Hedjazienne,
Paris, March 3, 1919.

Dear Mr. Frankfurter:
I want to take this opportunity of my first contact with American Zionists to tell you what I have often been able to say to Dr. Weizmann in Arabia and Europe.

We feel that the Arabs and Jews are cousins in race, having suffered similar oppressions at the hands of powers stronger than themselves, and by a happy coincidence have been able to take the first step towards the attainment of their national ideals together.

We Arabs, especially the educated among us, look with the deepest sympathy on the Zionist movement. Our deputation here in Paris is fully acquainted with the proposals submitted yesterday by the Zionist Organization to the Peace Conference, and we regard them as moderate and proper. We will do our best, in so far as we are concerned, to help them through: we will wish the Jews a most hearty welcome home.

With the chiefs of your movement, especially with Dr. Weizmann, we have had and continue to have the closest relations. He has been a great helper of our cause, and I hope the Arabs may soon be in a position to make the Jews some return for their kindness. We are working together for a reformed and revived Near East, and our two movements complete one another. The Jewish movement is national and not imperialist, and there is room in Syria for us both. Indeed, I think that neither can be a real success without the other. People less informed and less responsible than our leaders and yours, ignoring the need for cooperation of the Arabs and Zionists have been trying to exploit

190

the local difficulties that must necessarily arise in Palestine in the early stages of our movements. Some of them have, I am afraid, misrepresented your aims to the Arab peasantry, and our aims to the Jewish peasantry, with the result that interested parties have been able to make capital out of what they call our differences.

I wish to give you my firm conviction that these differences are not on questions of principle, but on matters of detail such as must inevitably occur in every contact of neighboring peoples, and are as easily adjusted by mutual goodwill. Indeed nearly all of them will disappear with fuller knowledge.

I look forward, and my people with me look forward, to a future in which we will help you and you will help us, so that the countries in which we are mutually interested may once again take their places in the community of civilized peoples of the world.

Believe me, Yours sincerely
(Sgd.) Feisal

Listen to the salutation to the dawn, Look to this day for it is life, the very life of life,
In its brief course lie all the verities and realities of our existence.
The bliss of growth, the splendour of beauty,
For yesterday is but a dream and tomorrow is only a vision,
But today well spent makes every yesterday a dream of happiness and every tomorrow a vision of hope.
Look well therefore to this day Such is the salutation to the dawn.
Sanskrit Salutation To The Dawn

Years have passed. The State of Israel is reborn and some Arab nations have achieved independence. Bitter misunderstandings, big-power intrigue, oil politics, terrorism, war and unmitigated suffering have poisoned

191

the friendship and hope shared by Arabs and Jews. Can it be restored? Why not? The far more endemic hatred and bloodshed of centuries between French and Germans, between Germans and Russians, between Indians and Pakistanis and between Japanese and Chinese have all given way to peaceful reconciliation in recent years.

The first step in the peace process was taken by the martyred President Anwar Sadat of Egypt and Prime Minister Menahem Begin of Israel, with energetic assistance from President Jimmy Carter of the United States. The extension of that process to embrace all Arab states in the area can open new horizons of hope for the whole international community. As in the past, the Near East is situated uniquely to be the bridge between East and West. To reconstruct that bridge, so vital to world peace and renewal in our time, challenges all the children of Abraham to a rapprochement of historic importance. Out of that family reunion, the renaissance of both national cultures and the cultural enrichment of all humanity can develop. . .which is, after all, a modern restatement of the old biblical promise to Abraham: "And all the nations of the world will be blessed in you and in your descendants."

All blessings flow from an honest confrontation of the truth. Abraham, who left his birthplace to make aliyah, to settle in the Holy Land, was the first Zionist. He is also the father of the Arab nation. That truth alone points the way to reconciliation and healing.

A near eastern scholar used to regale visitors to his home with this story: "How is it," he would ask, "that among all human languages, Hebrew and Arabic are unique in having one and the same word to connote both hello and goodbye — shalom in Hebrew and salaam in Arabic?" Nobody wanted to inform the professor that the Hawaiians also have such a word, aloha; that would obviously ruin his story. So they would humor him by playing straightmen: "Tell us, why is Hebrew and Arabic so unique?" And he would answer: "Because many Jews and Arabs don't know whether they are coming or going."

The mindless way of hit-and-run hostility is unworthy of Abraham's descendants. Two very wise and visionary statesmen, the late Emir Faisal ibn Hussein and Dr. Chaim Weitzmann, agreed upon a better way 60 years ago. The Emir's felicitous words can help both Jews and Arabs rediscover that way of mutual honor and blessing. They bear restatement:

> "We are working together for a reformed and revived Near East and our two movements complete one another. The Jewish movement is national and not imperialist. Our movement is national and not imperialist, and there is room in Syria (The Holy Land was then in the southern region of Syria) for us both. Indeed I think that neither can be a real success without the other."

We who have lost our sense and our senses - our touch, our smell, our vision of who we are, we who frantically force and press all things, without rest for body or spirit, hurting our earth and injuring ourselves: we call a halt.

We want to rest. We need to rest and allow the earth to rest. We need to reflect and to rediscover the mystery that lives in us, that is the ground of every unique expression of life, the source of the fascination that calls all things to communion.

We declare Sabbath, a space of quiet: for simply being and letting be, for recovering the great, forgotten truths, for learning how to live again. U.N. Enviromental Sabbath Program

One little Hebrew pronoun, a two letter word, prosaic and undistinguished, is your key here to the fourth dimension. A Kabbalistic comment of genius on that simple pronoun illumines the whole process of mystical communication with God via scripture.

The pronoun is "lecha - to you" and it's in Abraham's charge: "Lech lecha - Go forth." King James translates: "Get thee forth." So what's the problem? This dative pronoun, lecha, seems superfluous. The imperative, lech, already means go forth or get thee forth. Most translators and commentators take lecha to be an archaic appendage to the Hebrew imperative. But the mystics are not content to treat it as a mere literary idiom; for them, every biblical word is a vehicle of divine inspiration.

And so the masters of Zohar dig deeper and, in exploring beneath that one Hebrew pronoun, they uncover a resplendent new world of meaning. They understand the divine call, "Lech lecha," as "Go into yourself", Abraham, get to know yourself. God is instructing Abraham to embark on an immortal mission, to uproot himself and make the long trip from Mesopotamia to the Holy Land. But the fulfillment of his life's work requires more than a journey over the surface of the earth; he will first need to make the internal journey and get into his cells to discover who he really is.

That is the message God is communicating to Abraham: "Go forth into yourself. . .to the land that I will show you." The Kabbalists explain: "I will show you a land you have not yet experienced nor have you known the power of that region so deep and hidden within you." Clearly this message to Abraham speaks directly to us all. Whatever our purpose in life, our calling, our work — it cannot be fulfilled if we remain strangers to ourselves.

The story is told of the late Professor of Philosophy Morris Raphael Cohen whom a student in class once asked:

~ Dr. Cohen, how do I know I exist?

The sage snapped back:

~ Who's asking?

How many of us live out our lives barely knowing we exist, unaware of the infinite, vibrant, miraculous world within us waiting to be explored and developed? Strangers to ourselves, out of touch with our real inner strengths and latencies, we live with all the surface encrustations of doubt, fear, guilt, inadequacy and unworthiness that have been laid upon us from infancy. Those negative self-images we accept as real. We pronounce a harsh judgment upon ourselves day by day, sentencing ourselves to a life of frustration and bitterness.

What a cruel distortion of the life we were created to live! Those mystics of the Zohar struck pure gold in their inspired, fourth-dimensional grasp of Abraham's biblical calling, "Go forth...to the land that I will show you." They perceived the truth that God is telling everyone of us: get on with your life's journey...get into yourself and you will find a world within you that you never knew existed; nor could you conceive of its power for self-renewal.

What the Kabbalist intuited 600 years ago is the new frontier of modern research in all the life sciences. Never before have the inner mysteries of our human body been so intensively explored. The more deeply we probe into this miniature world-space of cells and genes, of substances and processes, the greater our amazement. Awesome power, exquisite complexity, vital energy and

195

infinite mystery — that's the real you! And all of it is delicately balanced within a self-sustaining unity, your own personal life-system. We are each of us a wondrous spark of cosmic unity and infinity. How can we settle for the life of a shlemiel?

And what of the hidden regions of our mind, those esoteric realms of our ideas and feelings, values and intuitions, dreams and imaginings, awareness and cognition, creativity and fulfillment? Pioneering expeditions into the galaxies of our brain are now producing the first crude maps for this vast area. This cartography will improve and so will our ability to use our deepest mental, emotional and spiritual resources — all of them dynamically interlaced within an organically unified field.

Don't wait for the final results, the perfect wisdom. The research is as infinite as the Cosmic Creator Himself and much of it beyond the competence of quantitative instrumentation. But the mystics were right. Lech lecha – get on with your life's journey into external and internal space. The fun is in the growing!

196

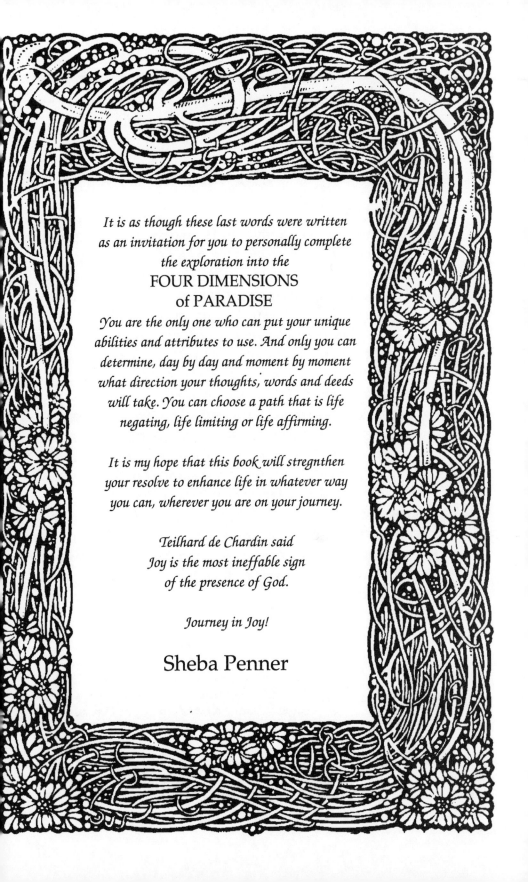

It is as though these last words were written
as an invitation for you to personally complete
the exploration into the
FOUR DIMENSIONS
of PARADISE
You are the only one who can put your unique
abilities and attributes to use. And only you can
determine, day by day and moment by moment
what direction your thoughts, words and deeds
will take. You can choose a path that is life
negating, life limiting or life affirming.

It is my hope that this book will stregnthen
your resolve to enhance life in whatever way
you can, wherever you are on your journey.

Teilhard de Chardin said
Joy is the most ineffable sign
of the presence of God.

Journey in Joy!

Sheba Penner

THE FAMILY OF MAN

A Prayer

GOD OF ALL NATIONS AND GOD OF ALL MEN, GIVE US THE WISDOM TO PERCEIVE THE MUTUALITY OF MANKIND; OPEN OUR MINDS AND HEARTS TO THE TRUTH WHICH CAN TELL US THAT THE ONLY RACE ON EARTH IS THE RACE OF THE LIVING; HELP US TO JOIN TOGETHER IN NOBILITY AND IN RESPECT THE PEOPLE OF ALL LANDS AND OF ALL COLORS IN A FAMILY OF HUMANITY. IN THIS OUR LIFE ON EARTH HELP US TO MAKE OF IT A TIME OF WORK, OF PEACE, OF PROGRESS. GIVE US THE UNDERSTANDING BY WHICH WE MAY KNOW GOOD FROM EVIL, AND THE COURAGE AND THE STRENGTH TO FORTIFY THE ONE AND TO DESTROY THE OTHER. GIVE US THE PERCEPTION TO SEE THE VASTNESS OF YOUR HANDIWORK, TO SEE IN THE SURROUNDING INFINITY ONE DESIGN AND ONE REASON THAT WILL GIVE US ONE BELIEF. GIVE US THE AWARENESS BY WHICH WE MAY LEARN AS ONE MAN THE DIGNITY AND REALITY OF A COMMON FAITH NURSED BY KNOWLEDGE INSTEAD OF IGNORANCE, BY INTEGRITY INSTEAD OF DECEIT, BY HOPE INSTEAD OF FEAR. GIVE US, O GOD, THE HIGHER INTELLIGENCE TO TELL US THAT THE EARTH WE STAND ON IS COMMON GROUND, AND GIVE US THE ONENESS OF PURPOSE AND VISION TO BUILD ON THAT GROUND A HOME OF ETERNAL FREEDOM.

— This prayer written and delivered on
Sunday, May 2nd, 1945, before a congregation
of all faiths at Norwalk, Conn., by Norman Cousins,
editor of The Saturday Review of Literature, on the
occasion of the observance of a Day of Compassion
for Jews victimized by Nazi persecution.

198

The only responsibility you cannot evade in this life is the one you probably think of least - your personal influence. Every moment of your life you are changing, to a degree, the life of the whole world...
Never be content to merely influence others with your radiation. Seek to be an inspiration, bringing out the best in others by radiating the best in yourself.

Power of Personal Influence
Adapted from "The Majesty of Calmness"
by William Jourdan, 1900

We leave traces of ourselves wherever we go, on whatever we touch.
Lewis Thomas, *The Life of a Cell*

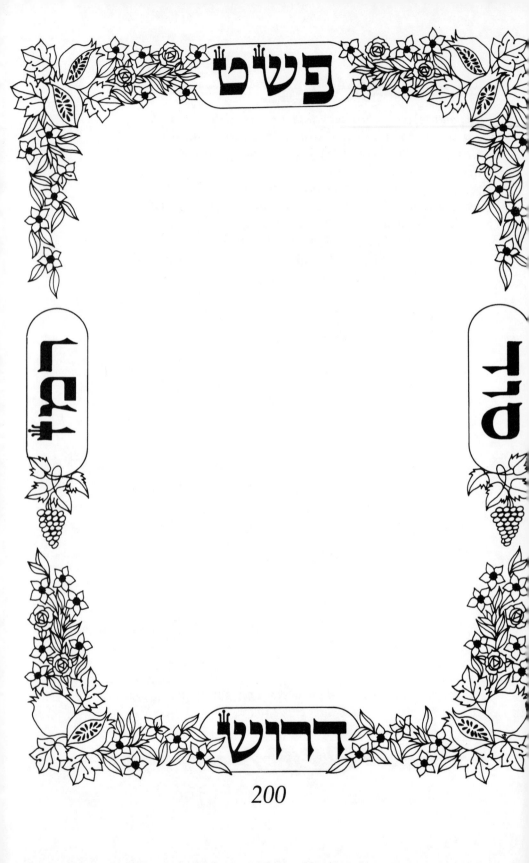

פשט

סוד

רמז

דרוש